THE

W...

OF

EVERYTHING

Don Lessem

McGRAW-HILL BOOK COMPANY

New York   St. Louis   San Francisco   Bogotá   Hamburg
Madrid   Mexico   Milan   Montreal   Panama   Paris
São Paolo   Singapore   Tokyo   Toronto

1 2 3 4 5 6 7 8 9 FGR FGR 8 9 0 9 8

ISBN 0-07-037473-2

Library of Congress Cataloging-in-Publication Data

Lessem, Don
   The worst of everything: the experts' listing of the most
loathsome and deficient in every realm of our lives / Don Lessem.
      p. cm.
   ISBN 0-07-037473-2
   1. Curiosities and wonders.   2. World records.   I. Title.
AG243.L42 1988
031'.02—dc19   87–31043
                                                          CIP

Book design by Eve Kirch

THE

WORST

OF

EVERYTHING

The Experts' Listing of the Most Loathsome and Deficient in Every Realm of Our Lives

For Maggie Manning—
The best there was at seeing
the worst and best in literature and life.

ACKNOWLEDGMENTS

This book would not have been possible without all those who have contributed their bile, or the U.S. Postal Service (Harvard, Massachusetts, branch), a persistent agent, a visionary editor, and a forbearing wife and children. Yes, all these exist. So, thank you, my contributors, Dick, Trish and Gerry, Al Zuckerman, Tom Miller, Paula Hartstein, and Rebecca and Erica (a.k.a. Lucy Mouse) Lessem. Go blame them.

CONTENTS

ENTERTAINMENT AND CELEBRITY WORSTS

SPORTS WORSTS

Worsts in Professional Baseball

Worsts in Professional Basketball

Worsts in College Basketball

Worsts in Professional Football

Worsts in Professional Ice Hockey

BUSINESS AND POLITICAL WORSTS

Worsts in Business

Worsts in Politics

DEATH AND DESTRUCTION WORSTS

PREFACE

Before addressing the worst in life, one question must be asked: Hasn't this book already been written?

The answer is no, to the surprise of followers of that highly derivative genre, the list book. So in the spirit of public education and personal enrichment I offer yet another list book. Those who don't share the enthusiasm Joseph McCarthy, David Wallechinsky, and I have had for keeping lists are urged to buzz off. And a "see ya later" to those who consider bad news no news and its mavens just nattering nabobs of negativism.

The rest of you, come on in. You'll find an antipasto of antipathies gathered from supposedly reliable reference sources and respected, if crotchety, critics. The latter represent the most soft-hearted, and perhaps -headed, of the hundreds of prominent types who were asked to submit their personal purgatories.

We've essayed wherever possible to avoid repetition, but some names—Sylvester Stallone and Andy Rooney chief among them—keep showing up. Nothing personal, boys, but if there is a Worst of the Worst, you take the crumb cake. There is, however, plenty of vilification to go around.

There is not, however, space for ample thanks to all who have contributed. This book represents many hours of research on the part of many people, and a bit of envelope licking on my own part. Special thanks go to all contributors, since they won't be getting a penny from royalties or the film rights.

But particular hosannas to editor Tom Miller and agent Al Zuckerman for their splendid taste in book proposals, to sports researcher nonpareil Ron Sataloff, to disaster man James Cornell, and to my wife and children for staying out of the basement while I typed.

Don Lessem

The basement
December 7, 1987

LIFE STYLE
WORSTS

We know you have your problems, but it could be worse. You could be commuting to work in New York City (an 80-minute ordeal), running low on gas in your Rolls-Royce (8 miles per gallon), sending your children to school in Pascagoula, or having them drop out in El Paso. You could be planning a vacation to India or, closer to home, Atlantic City. Or planning a family with siblings spaced less than 3 years apart. Or buying a ruffled tuxedo shirt, going on the Stillman diet, or letting the theft insurance on your Rabbit convertible lapse.

You could be looking for a dentist in Pierre or a television set in Bangladesh. You could be buying eggs in Melbourne, a burger in Kyoto, or a vacuum cleaner in Bogotá. You could be looking for a job in Newark, NJ, or a husband in Garland, TX.

It's nice to know that however bad you have it, somewhere, somehow, someone has it worse. Just who, how, and where, we will now reveal in detail. Keep your pencil handy and start those cards and letters coming in. Tell us about your operation—or send notes of sympathy to the taxpayers of Stockholm and the job seekers of Glasgow.

I Say It's Liver and I Hate It

The 3 Most Hated Foods

1. Tofu

2. Liver

3. Yogurt

—From survey data of the Roper Organization.

Here we have obviously only the cream of the crap. What about anchovies, pimentos, persimmons, those foods (for good reason) out of the ordinary American diet? And we're not talking about prepared foods, so we can't dwell on chipped beef, prize-winning jello and cornflake recipes, or foods that may not even be foods, like Spam and imitation sausage. Still, incomplete as this listing is, we find it reassuring. It's a sign that trend-

iness hasn't overtaken the country (see #1), nor has the diet craze (see #3). And the food we most loved to hate as children hasn't lost its power to disgust yet another generation, the high vitamin content of organ meats notwithstanding. Call it paté, call it summer steak, it is just plain loathsome. If parents would heed these findings, one of childhood's worst tortures could be averted. It is with just such public service in mind that I took on this project.

Eat, Drink, and Be Very Sick

The 10 Worst Foods in the Common American Diet, According to Jane Brody

FRENCH FRIES—Two hundred calories of fat plus salt added to an otherwise nutritious, nearly fat- and salt-free 100-calorie potato

CHEESE—Fattier, saltier, and more caloric than red meat, ironically consumed in vast amounts as a meat substitute by the health-conscious

PATÉ—A heart attack's best friend, meant only for those with Drano in their blood vessels

PASTA SALAD—Another desecration of a healthy food, achieved by drowning it in a dressing laden with fat and salt

GRANOLA BARS—Expensive cookies with a healthful image that belies the fact that their main ingredients are fat and sugar

S'MORES CRUNCH—One of the newest and by far the worst of sugar cereals, with more than half the calories from sugar; even turns the milk brown

HOT DOGS—Eighty-five percent of calories from fat, plus meat you'd never otherwise eat, salt, nitrites, and nitrates

BACON—Really fat, not meat, plus oodles of salt and cancer-promoting nitrates and nitrites

SODA POP—With or without real sugar, a wholly artificial nutritional travesty; a very expensive way to drink water, the only ingredient of value

POTATO CHIPS—Three hundred calories of fat plus salt added to an otherwise nutritious, nearly fat- and salt-free 100-calorie potato

—Special to *The Worst of Everything* from Jane Brody, author and nutrition writer for the *New York Times*.

In other words, if it tastes good it will kill you. Don't eat to live, live to eat, our grandmothers told us. Come to find out, it's eat to die. But all in all, it's a better route to the common destination than kissing a truck or taking 5000 rads.

Eat to Die

The 7 Worst Diets, According to Dian White

1. THE BEVERLY HILLS DIET—Six weeks of pineapple, pineapple, and more pineapple. Who wouldn't get sick of eating?

2. THE STILLMAN DIET—And all the other high-protein, low-carbohydrate diets, which can give you kidney stones, bone loss, and an insatiable craving for broccoli.

3. THE BROWN RICE DIET—That's all you eat, brown rice. In this case too much of a good thing really isn't enough. Some people dieted themselves to death on this one.

4. THE CAMBRIDGE DIET—This regimen also underscored the "die" in diet for an unfortunate few.

5. THE LIQUID PROTEIN DIET—Yet another potential killer.

6. THE REACH-FOR-YOUR-MATE-INSTEAD-OF-YOUR-PLATE DIET—Here sex is a substitute for food. But what if sex makes you hungry?

7. THE IT'S NOT-YOUR-FAULT-YOU'RE-FAT DIET—So whose fault is it?

—Special to *The Worst of Everything* from Dian White, syndicated lifestyle columnist of the *Boston Globe*.

Personally, I say no diet is dangerous, since none has ever been adhered to, judging by what adheres to most Americans. Fat is not only the norm (see Cheers), it is the shape of evolution. Nature gave us a sweet tooth (perhaps to recognize ripe fruit, something I still can't do at the supermarket without putting my thumb through the cantaloupe). The sweet tooth, opposable thumb, and large brain led to things like making, buying, and holding firmly onto Dove Bars, which leads directly to fat.

You're Not Just Fat, You're Stupid

The 25 Dumbest Diet Blunders

1. Blaming your frame

2. Not exercising

3. Cutting back to 500 calories a day or fasting

4. Pigging out prior to a diet

5. Being seduced by the salad bar

6. Cutting out snacks

7. Using laxatives or diuretics to induce weight loss

8. Not taking multivitamins while dieting

9. Eating only one food, especially if that food is protein

10. Having an on-off diet mentality

11. Using liquid diets

12. Weighing yourself every day

13. Expecting to lose weight too quickly

14. Dieting for someone else

15. Believing that food allergies make you fat

16. Ordering the diet plate

17. Relying on diet pills or diet aids

18. Skipping meals

19. Eliminating carbohydrates

20. Thinking you can't feel great while dieting

21. Having a frozen body image

22. Always feeling too fat

23. Swearing off sweets

24. Relying solely on calorie count to select foods

25. Not giving yourself enough time to purchase, prepare, and eat food

---

—From *Glamour*, January 1986.

And let's not forget eating only on days with an "r" in them, locking your refrigerator, opening your appendectomy scar to insert a vacuum cleaner, amputating digits, and, worst of all, eating liver.

Gallows for Ernest & Julio

The Most Overrated Wines, According to
Paul Zimmerman

1. MOUTON CADET—It has the Rothschild name and little else.

2. MOREAU BLANC—It's been bad since they took the chardonnay out of the blend 5 years ago.

3. JOSEPH DROUHIN BURGUNDIES—I've tasted 2 good ones in the last 7 years.

4. GALLO HEARTY BURGUNDY—It's fine if you like cherry syrup.

5. NOZDROVIC BRUT RUSSIAN CHAMPAGNE—The "brut" should have an "e" after it.

—Special to *The Worst of Everything* from Paul Zimmerman, former wine critic of the *New York Post*.

What, no Thunderbird! No Bali Hai? Paul and I don't shop in the same stores, I take it. I suspect the American taste for alcohol still runs closer to imbibing cough syrup when a 6-pack isn't available than to looking for the right year of some naive domestic or an import with a good nose. Away from the coasts, oenophilia is still seen as just another continental perversion —I'll wager my last bottle of nectarine-flavored wine cooler on it.

Eat It and Weep

The Worst in Food, 1987, According to John F. Mariani

MOST OVERDESIGNED RESTAURANT—Kate Mantilini in Los Angeles. It looks like a luncheonette designed by the Terminator.

SMALLEST TREND—Mini fast food like Kentucky Fried's 1-ounce Chicken Littles, Popeye's 2-ounce Little Chickadees, and Burger King's 1-ounce Burger Bundles.

WORST NEW COOKIE—Chocolate-covered Oreos

WORST NEW EATERY—Sam's Cafe, New York City. Mariel Hemingway's third venture into old-fashioned U.S.A. food—like pasty crabcakes, tasteless sirloins, bland chickens.

—From *USA Today*, December 6, 1987.

You Didn't Get That Thing at Neiman-Marcus

The 4 Worst Fashion Items, According to
Stanley Marcus

1. Ruffled tuxedo shirts

2. Filigreed metal dressing-table accessories

3. Metal brocade tuxedo jackets

4. Any tuxedo jacket made for women

—Special to *The Worst of Everything* from Stanley Marcus, president and chief executive officer, Neiman-Marcus.

Frankly, I don't get anything at Neiman-Marcus except vertigo when I see the price tags. The guys I admire don't wear any shirts with their tuxedos (how do you think Butch Lewis got to be such a great fight promoter?) and I'm not sure what filigree is, but it sure sounds bad to me. Ditto for brocade. Women should not be wearing men's clothes, as Mr. Marcus or anyone in the clothing business will tell you, or they are liable to find out that, while immensely more boring, they are a quantum leap closer to being reasonably priced and sturdily made than the cheesecloth Mondo Bizarro attire that passes for feminine fashion. I don't know why Mr. Marcus has tuxedos so much in mind, unless he goes to a lot of proms or penguin rookeries.

No, Honey, That's Not a Lipstick Mark

The 6 Worst Things to Do in Marriage, According to Dr. Joyce Brothers

1. BEING UNFAITHFUL TO YOUR MATE—Physical infidelity is the worst thing you can do, even if your spouse never finds out. The break in trust builds a wall very difficult to break down.

2. NOT REVEALING YOUR INTIMATE SECRETS—Everyone has his or her own sexual and emotional fantasies, infidelities, and jealousies. These secrets of marriage must be shared.

3. BEING MANIPULATED BY YOUR CHILDREN—Don't let them cause you to reverse your mate's stand on discipline. If Mommy says "can't," then Daddy should say "can't."

4. WALKING OUT ON A QUARREL—This is the worst way to end an argument.

5. SPENDING DISCRETIONARY MONEY UNWISELY—Not agreeing on or not telling your spouse in advance about using money for other than basic services and recreation can be a major source of trouble.

6. ANNOYING PERSONAL HABITS—Small, annoying things callously done—like falling asleep in front of the TV set or drying panty hose on the shower rod—can build up like the Chinese water torture.

—Special to *The Worst of Everything* from Dr. Joyce Brothers, psychologist, author, commentator.

Dr. Brothers' list may read like a wish list for many of us. Certainly it is intriguing to consider how many of the above sins one might commit, even combine—as in yelling at your spouse for leaving her toenail clippings in the bed, then walking out, picking up a prostitute with your grocery money, and later rushing home to give your son the car keys. Should you tell the wife you gave away the keys and the grocery money or wait until she discovers you've contracted a communicable disease? Marriage is indeed a complex business.

Forget about Pimples and Car Keys

The 6 Worst Problems Facing Teens, According to "Ask Beth"

1. Not being liked by that certain boy or girl (by far the most frequently asked problem)

2. Being asked out and your parents won't let you go

3. Deciding whether or not to try pot when your friends use it

4. Knowing whether it's OK to go without underwear (tops for girls, bottoms for boys)

5. Wanting to break up but not wanting to hurt your friend's feelings

6. Wondering how far (sexually) is far enough

—Special to *The Worst of Everything* from Beth Winship, syndicated advice columnist, "Ask Beth."

Lucky Beth. All the teens I hear about never think of wearing underwear or of asking their parents anything. The decisions which seem to perplex them are principally which drug to ingest and which felony to commit on any given afternoon of truancy. Then again, it's all pretty much what I recall hearing about my own generation when I was a teen. The answer, I think, is for teenagers to get their own congressional lobby and a press agent; maybe the same one who has convinced so many people that Richard Gere is an actor.

Children Should Be Seen and...,

*The 3 Worst Ages for Children, According
to Dr. Burton White*

1. BIRTH TO 10 WEEKS—Babies do not ordinarily sleep
   through the night. They have a cry like chalk going up a
   blackboard. It's normal to dislike your infant intensely at
   3 a.m.

2. FROM 15–17 MONTHS TO 21–22 MONTHS—A normal phase
   of negativism begins when the child comes to realize it
   has some power. For 5 or 6 months, children will try out
   the power to refuse. This "no, no, no" period is a preview
   of adolescence.

3. OLDER CHILD UNDER 3½ AND YOUNGER CHILD OVER 7
   MONTHS—Signs of jealousy and aggression appear in the
   older child, especially if he or she was overindulged before the second child's birth. As a parent you're in the
   soup. But try and consider how you'd feel if your wife
   said she was bringing home another man, someone younger, to live with you, and she was going to give him more
   attention. It's not surprising then that negativism doesn't
   go away in the older child, but intensifies. The smaller
   the age gap, the more the potential for a nightmarish
   problem.

—Special to *The Worst of Everything* from Dr. Burton White, psychologist,
former professor at the Harvard School of Education, and author of *The First
Three Years of Life*.

*I will attest personally to the veracity of Dr. White's obser-
vations. I might, however, have changed the wording to read,
"It's normal to want to express-mail your child to Novosibirsk at
3 a.m., send him on a ride in the trash compacter when he becomes colicky...and put him in a maximum-security prison when
sibling rivalry rears its ugly head." The comforting thought, also
not expressed above, for all parents experiencing such ordeals, is
that the problems will pass soon enough. Then you can settle back
and begin saving for bail bond, $100,000-a-year college tuition,*

and the other expenses of teen years, when all these behaviors will be repeated with the volume turned up.

Tune In, Turn On, Drop Out

The 12 Worst Problems in Public Schools

	%Times Cited
1. Lack of discipline	25
2. Use of drugs	18
3. Poor curriculum	11
4. Difficulty getting good teachers	10
5. Lack of financial support	9
6. Pupils' lack of interest/truancy	5
6. Large schools/overcrowding	5
8. Integration/busing	4
8. Teachers' lack of interest	4
10. Drinking/alcoholism	3
10. Parent's lack of interest	3
10. Lack of input by teachers and students	3

—From a 1985 Gallup Poll.

This is a fine list as far as it goes. But I wonder just what is embraced by "lack of discipline." At present, as we all know, teachers regularly mete out such draconian punishments as taking away amphetamines for the rest of the period, reducing automatic As to automatic B+s, and making those who miss more than three-fourths of all classes ineligible for valedictorian status. What kind of sanctions do the martinets who cry for more discipline have in mind? Capital punishment? A reasonable deterrent, methinks, to be used only in cases of extremely poor handwriting. Capital punishment of another sort—forfeiture of $50 weekly allowance or keys to the Stingray—might be just as effective. Take out that whip, mentors, and let's get cracking. There is still no substitute for the three Rs— rasslin', ropin', and roughin' up.

A Loose Upper Lip

The 5 Worst American Preconceptions about the British, According to Alistair Cooke

1. They are all upper- or upper-middle class—if they are not cockneys or coal miners.

2. Their food is inferior to American food.

3. They are less democratic than Americans. (This preconception is based on a misunderstanding of the role of the powerless constitutional monarchy.)

4. Their popular press is not the worst in the world.

5. They are "class-riddled." In fact, since the Second World War they have undergone a more radical social revolution than the Americans, among whom the absolutely top social class is still the plutocracy.

—Special to *The Worst of Everything* from Alistair Cooke, author, critic, and commentator.

To which we might add: no sense of humor, bad teeth, a heartless reactionary fossil of a leader, and a moribund economy. Wait a minute, is that them or us?

Vive la Différence

The 2 Worst American Misconceptions about the French, According to Pierre Salinger

1. They hate Americans. They don't hate Americans. The fact is the majority of French people are very pro-American.* The problem is that most tourists go only to places such as Paris and not into the countryside, where the pro-American sentiment is strongest.

2. Theirs is a country of only gastronomy, wine, perfume, and haute couture. France is, in fact, one of the leading high-tech countries in the world. In the last 10 years they've

developed the world's fastest train, and the Parisian telephone system places a computer in every home.

*According to a 1986 French public opinion poll, Ronald Reagan was the
most popular foreign leader. France is, it should also be noted, the nation
that considers Jerry Lewis not only an entertainer but an artist. Plainly, the
Gallic capacity for self-delusion is unmatched, even by their lust for spiced
goose fat, squashed old grapes, and each other.

—Special to *The Worst of Everything* from Pierre Salinger, author, former
presidential press secretary, and chief of ABC's Paris news bureau.

Wish You Weren't Here

*The 12 Worst Countries to Visit, According to
Michael Carlton*

1. INDIA—Too poor, too dusty, too dirty, too much curry.

2. CHINA—The crowds are tremendous and the people spit
   on the sidewalks, making a street crossing in Shanghai a
   little like the Ice Capades.

3. GREECE—The women have mustaches and the men smell
   of goat cheese.

4. EGYPT—If watching people urinate against the side of a
   pyramid is your idea of fun, you'll love Egypt.

5. RUSSIA—The Russians are the rudest people on earth.
   The toughness evidenced in their behavior is exceeded
   only by the toughness of their meat, which is gray and
   inedible.

6. NEW ZEALAND—They don't like our bombs; I don't like
   their food, their hotels, or their boring countryside, which
   may be beautiful but will put you to sleep after a few
   hours of watching sheep after sheep after....

7. MEXICO—Mañana has become mañana maybe. And only
   if you tip well. Their big resorts are like Miami Beach,
   only without the charm.

8. ARUBA—The world's ugliest island, this place is so devoid of anything to do that even Gilligan would flee. With its casinos, it is like Las Vegas, only without the charm (see Mexico above).

9. SOUTH AFRICA—A beautiful country has been sullied by riots, foolish racial policies, and fear.

10. PANAMA—There is only one climate, hot, and only one temperament, hotter. You couldn't pick a better place to get into a knife fight.

11. NEW GUINEA—They eat people here. And if the natives don't get you, the snakes probably will.

12. KOREA—People here eat raw garlic. Isn't that reason enough to avoid the place?

———

—Special to *The Worst of Everything* from Michael Carlton, syndicated travel columnist of the *Denver Post*.

I don't know about you but I love this guy. Xenophobia is a great American tradition. I think we've got a new U.N. ambassador in the making here.

Just Passing Through

The 5 Worst Travel Attractions in the Western Hemisphere, According to William Davis

1. THE GLASS FLOWERS, HARVARD UNIVERSITY, CAMBRIDGE, MA—Unless you are seriously into botany or are a glass-blowing freak, this is a profoundly unexciting attraction housed in the bowels of a museum which is itself a fusty monument to nineteenth-century museumship.

2. TIDAL BORE, MONCTON, NEW BRUNSWICK, CANADA—The Bore is one. It was once an imposing wall of water which rolled up the Petitcodiac River whenever the tide (the world's highest) from the Bay of Fundy rushed in. But

because of alterations in the tidal pattern, caused by construction of causeways and landfills, the Bore is now a barely perceptible ripple on the surface of the river.

3. FLOATING GARDENS OF XOCHIMILCO, MEXICO CITY —Once a charming spot surrounded by flower and produce gardens, Xochimilco has been engulfed in the last decade by the urban monster that is Mexico City, with disastrous results. The area's flower gardens are long gone, and the many boats that carry tourists and maniacally strumming mariachis through the canals are nowadays decorated with paper and plastic posies. The water table has fallen so much that the trees lining the canals are dying because their roots are exposed. The canals themselves are green with pollution and carpeted with floating trash. It is a scene only a tourist guide could love.

4. TOP OF THE MARK, SAN FRANCISCO—In its '40s heyday, the bar atop the Mark Hopkins Hotel, with its panoramic view of the Golden Gate Bridge and the bay, was the "in" place in San Francisco. Time and an expanding skyline have passed it by. Unless you are nostalgic or an old movie buff, or both, what it now offers is an obstructed view, rather pricey drinks, and the opportunity to pick up a nostalgic widow from the midwest who likes old movies.

5. TIMES SQUARE, NEW YORK CITY—Although somewhat less sleazy than formerly, Times Square—the traditional heart of Manhattan—is still tawdry, tacky, and depressing, while some of the streets around it are incredibly sordid and frequently dangerous. A disgrace.

—Special to *The Worst of Everything* from William Davis, senior travel writer for the *Boston Globe*.

Be it ever so humble, there's no place like home. And we're talking humble. As a frequent visitor to the Glass Flowers exhibit (regrettably, it lies in the path to the fine library of the Mu-

seum of Comparative Zoology at Harvard), I can attest to the remarkable narcolepsy-inducing effect of even a pass-through. The exhibit was organized by George Plimpton's grandfather, which may account for the grandson's desire to carry on the same effect in literature. Can't say I've been to Moncton. And if I haven't been there yet, I'll be darn sure not to go now.

Wish You Were Here Instead of Me

The 9 Most Overrated American Tourist Attractions, According to Steve Birnbaum

1. ATLANTIC CITY—It's no more than a stage set; it has no style, no substance.

2. MYRTLE BEACH—It's the tacky capital of the east coast.

3. NIAGARA FALLS—It takes a pair of blinders to shut out all the shabby surroundings.

4. LAS VEGAS—It's a fine place to study the inspired uses of polyester.

5. CONEY ISLAND—Risking your life here for a hot dog is hard to justify.

6. PANAMA CITY, FL—It's the tacky capital of the gulf coast.

7. LOS ANGELES—It's the tacky capital of the west coast.

8. MIAMI BEACH—It's a monument to greed and bad taste; there's not even a little gaudy glitter anymore.

9. MOUNT RUSHMORE—It's a long way to go for 4 bad stone faces.

—Special to *The Worst of Everything* from Stephen Birnbaum, travel book writer, editor of *Diversion* and *Esquire,* and *Good Morning, America* travel editor.

Down Country

The 16 Least Comfortable Nations on Earth

	Rating*
1. Mozambique	95
2. Angola	91
3. Afghanistan	88
3. Chad	88
3. Mali	88
4. Ghana	87
4. Somalia	87
5. Niger	85
6. Burkina Faso	84
6. Central African Republic	84
6. Zaire	84
7. Benin	83
7. Malawi	83
8. Guinea	82
8. Ethiopia	82
8. Togo	82

*Nations are ranked according to a "human suffering index," an index of 10 factors including GNP, infant mortality, energy consumption and literacy rates, the availability of clean drinking water, and guaranteed human rights. Switzerland was rated most comfortable, followed by West Germany, Luxembourg, the Netherlands, and the United States.

—From a 1987 survey of 130 nations by the Population Crisis Committee of Washington, D.C.

"Comfortable" is one heck of a delicate euphemism here. I can think of many words for the lifestyle of the poor and neglected in these nations, but "uncomfortable" is not that high on the list. Then again, famine, disease, and death can be disconcerting. At least these people don't have to entertain Robin Leach. There's always a silver lining.

Anybody Home?

The 10 Least Crowded Cities on Earth

		People/Sq Mi
1.	Perth	447
2.	Santiago	676
3.	Lagos	791
4.	Brisbane	1556
5.	Melbourne	1666
6.	Manama	1987
7.	Edmonton	2040
8.	Sydney	2086
9.	Istanbul	2151
10.	Ankara	2279

—From John T. Marlin, Immanuel Ness, and Stephen T. Collins, *Book of World City Rankings,* Free Press, New York, 1986.

We could come up with slightly different figures if they'd let us schedule some special events in these and other cities—e.g., a Love-In in Beirut, an Honor Menachem Begin Parade through Tehran, or a Dry Monday in Melbourne, Moscow, or Paris.

Move Over, Will Ya?

The 10 Most Crowded Cities on Earth

		People/Sq Mi
1.	Manila	108,699
2.	Shanghai	70,449
3.	Cairo	63,373
4.	Paris	53,389
5.	Bombay	48,396
6.	Buenos Aires	37,959
7.	Seoul	35,755
8.	Osaka	32,137

9. Tokyo	29,874
10. Naples	26,942

—From John T. Marlin, Immanuel Ness, and Stephen T. Collins, *Book of World City Rankings*, Free Press, New York, 1986.

Turn Head and Cough

*The 10 Worst Countries in Which to Be a Conscientious Objector**

		Armed Forces/ 1000 Population
1.	Israel	43.4
2.	Cuba	39.1
3.	North Korea	37.1
4.	Vietnam	30.0
5.	Syria	28.4
6.	Taiwan	26.1
7.	Qatar	25.0
8.	Singapore	23.8
9.	Nicaragua	20.0
10.	Bulgaria	18.2

*For comparison, the U.S. has 9.1 people under arms per 1000 population, and the U.S.S.R. has 16.2.

—From the U.S. Arms Control and Disarmament Agency.

Question: What do the Swiss do with their conscientious objectors? Do they send them to the Vatican? Do they put them to work on Ollie North's accounts? Have them make chocolate soldiers? This is shaping up to be another of those "none of the above" answers. The statistics are deceptive, I think, as many of these nations are not only building up their armies by prescription but are taking a harder route toward influencing the ratio— that is, they're decimating the civilian population, often with products made in the U.S.A. I shudder to think how our balance of payments would look if no one were buying our weapons.

Nothing to Watch

The 10 Worst Countries in Which to Borrow a TV Set*

		Sets/1000 Population
1.	Bangladesh	1
1.	Ethiopia	1
3.	Sri Lanka	2
3.	India	2
5.	Kenya	4
5.	Kampuchea	4
5.	China	4
8.	Ghana	5
8.	Madagascar	5
8.	Nigeria	5

*The best—if you can call it that—place to find a TV set is in the U.S., where there are 624 sets per 1000 people. Japan has "only" 539 per 1000.

—From the U.N. Statistical Office.

Where Does It Hurt? Who Cares?

The 10 Major U.S. Cities with the Fewest Physicians*

		Physicians
1.	Pierre, SD	17
2.	Juneau, AK	27
3.	Montpelier, VT	41
4.	Carson City, NV	61
5.	Frankfort, KY	66
6.	Dover, DE	67

7.	Sterling Heights, MI	75
8.	Jefferson City, MO	77
9.	Helena, MT	78
10.	Chesapeake, VA	89

*The 199 largest cities in the United States were surveyed.

—From *199 American Cities Compared,* Information Publications, Burlington, VT, 1984 (U.S. Census, 1980).

Perhaps they make house calls in these places. And the temptation is just too great. The doctor gets in the car, drives through town, and just keeps going.

The Worst Places to Eat Caramels

The 10 Major U.S. Cities with the Fewest Dentists

		Dentists
1.	Pierre, SD	6
2.	Montpelier, VT	12
3.	Juneau, AK	13
4.	Carson City, NV	14
5.	Frankfort, KY	20
6.	Augusta, ME	24
7.	Chesapeake, VA	26
8.	Helena, MT	29
9.	Gary, IN	32
10.	Jefferson City, MO	33

—From *199 American Cities Compared,* Information Publications, Burlington, VT, 1984 (U.S. Census, 1980).

While the absence of dentists does have its obvious drawbacks, particularly after an encounter with a Charleston Chew, nevertheless it is taken by many as a distinct plus. Including me; my father is one.

If You Live Here, Move

The 10 Worst U.S. Metropolitan Areas*

1. Yuba City, CA

2. Pine Bluff, AK

3. Modesto, CA

4. Dothan, AL

5. Albany, GA

6. Benton Harbor, MI

7. Gadsden, AL

8. Casper, WY

9. Rockford, IL

10. Anderson, IN

*Criterion used is a cumulative rating of climate, arts, transportation, housing, economics, recreation, crime, health care, and education.

—From Richard Boyer and David Savageau, *Places Rated Almanac*, Rand McNally, Chicago, 1985.

Listed below are several analyses of specific and general reasons to avoid much of the urban U.S. If you can't take a measure of civic pride in noting that a city near you ranks high in something which, if you yourself accomplished it, would get your picture on a post office wall.

I'll Take Manhattan or Even Bristol

The 25 Worst Cities in America, According to Prof. Robert Pierce*

1. Fresno, CA

2. Lawrence, MA

3. Fitchburg, MA

4. Lawton, OK

5. Stockton, CA

6. Pine Bluff, AR

7. Texarkana, TX

8. Rockford, IL

9. Lowell, MA

10. Paterson, NJ

11. Great Falls, MT

12. Bakersfield, CA

13. Jackson, MI

14. Macon, GA

15. St. Joseph, MO

16. Lewiston, ME

17. Bristol, CT

18. New Britain, CT

19. Gary, IN

20. Meriden, CT

21. Waterbury, CT

22. Peoria, IL

23. Kankakee, IL

24. Corpus Christi, TX

25. Pittsfield, MA

*Based on a differential weighting of statistical lifestyle factors, according to a sample of the population's preferences for 277 cities.

—From Robert M. Pierce, State University of New York at Cortland, 1975.

Professor Pierce is a serious student of urban life. And he works in Cortland, NY. There is a definite connection to be made, I think. Personally, I'm wondering how I came to have the dubious distinction of living within a half-hour's drive of no less than 3 of the 10 worst American cities (#2, #3, and #9). Which way to run? I'm bound to approach one if I head west or north and to the south is Worcester, which deserves at least honorable mention here. To the east is Boston, full of beans, Celtics fans, and cod-eating Cabots. Fresno's looking better and better.

Stall and Crawl

*The 11 U.S. Metropolitan Areas with the Worst Commutes to Work**

	Min Daily
1. New York, NY	81.0
2. Nassau-Suffolk, NY	70.6
3. Washington, DC, MD, VA	64.5
4. Monmouth-Ocean Counties, NJ	64.0
5. Chicago, IL	63.8
6. Houston, TX	58.5
7. Baltimore, MD	58.3
8. Jersey City, NJ	57.6
9. Philadelphia, PA, NJ	56.3
10. New Orleans, LA	55.9
10. Newark, NJ	55.9

*Based on 1980 data—journey to work×2.2 to estimate round-trip minutes.

—From Richard Boyer and David Savageau, *Places Rated Almanac*, Rand McNally, Chicago, 1985.

You Can't Get There from Here

*The 20 Worst U.S. Metropolitan Areas
for Transportation**

1. Houma-Thibodaux, LA
2. Florence, AL
3. Steubenville-Weirton, OH, WV
4. Greeley, CO
5. Bremerton, WA
6. Pine Bluff, AR
7. Bloomington, IN
8. Pascagoula, MS
9. Jacksonville, NC
10. Kokomo, IN
11. Yuba City, CA
12. Athens, GA
13. Burlington, NC
14. Sherman-Denison, TX
15. Odessa, TX
16. Modesto, CA
17. Sharon, PA
18. McAllen-Edinburg-Mission, TX
19. Nassau-Suffolk, NY
20. Fort Pierce, FL

*Criteria used are daily commute, public transportation, interstate highways, air service, and passenger rail service.

—From Richard Boyer and David Savageau, *Places Rated Almanac*, Rand McNally, Chicago, 1985.

Hill Street Blues

The 10 U.S. Cities with the Most Crimes per Year

		Crimes/Yr
1.	New York, NY	688,567
2.	Los Angeles, CA	320,372
3.	Chicago, IL	181,891
4.	Houston, TX	166,063
5.	Detroit, MI	152,962
6.	Dallas, TX	115,684
7.	Philadelphia, PA	94,641
8.	Phoenix, AZ	75,654
9.	Boston, MA	74,039
10.	Baltimore, MD	72,911

—From *199 American Cities Compared*, Information Publications, Burlington, VT, 1984 (U.S. Census, 1980).

If It Isn't Nailed Down

The 15 Most Crime-Ridden U.S. Metropolitan Areas

		Score*
1.	New York, NY	2498
2.	Miami-Hialeah, FL	2459
3.	Los Angeles–Long Beach, CA	1960
4.	Las Vegas, NV	1913
5.	Atlantic City, NJ	1878
6.	West Palm Beach–Boca Raton–Delray Beach, FL	1783
7.	Baltimore, MD	1730
8.	Odessa, TX	1698
9.	Orlando, FL	1671

9.	Flint, MI	1671
11.	Gainesville, FL	1658
12.	San Francisco, CA	1619
13.	Savannah, GA	1614
14.	Lubbock, TX	1608
15.	New Orleans, LA	1604

*Score is sum of violent crime rate and one-tenth property crime rate.

—From Richard Boyer and David Savageau, *Places Rated Almanac,* Rand McNally, Chicago, 1985.

Easy to Be Cruel

The 10 U.S. Cities with the Most Violent Crimes per Year

		Violent Crimes*/Yr
1.	New York, NY	143,443
2.	Los Angeles, CA	53,957
3.	Chicago, IL	26,404
4.	Detroit, MI	23,746
5.	Philadelphia, PA	17,509
6.	Baltimore, MD	16,683
7.	Houston, TX	16,658
8.	Washington, DC	13,397
9.	Dallas, TX	13,053
10.	San Francisco, CA	11,706

*"Violent crimes" include murder, rape and attempted rape, aggravated assault (with intent to murder or injure), and robbery (theft with threat to injure).

—From *199 American Cities Compared,* Information Publications, Burlington, VT, 1984 (U.S. Census, 1980).

Next Stop, Reno

The 10 Worst Cities on Earth
for Staying Married In

		Divorce/ 1000 People
1.	Dallas	8.4
2.	Phoenix	7.8
3.	Houston	7.7
4.	Washington	7.0
5.	Leningrad	5.9
6.	San Diego	5.8
7.	San Francisco	5.5
8.	Kiev	5.3
9.	Los Angeles	5.2
10.	Baltimore	4.9

—From John T. Marlin, Immanuel Ness, and Stephen T. Collins, *Book of World City Rankings*, Free Press, New York, 1986.

Some surprising results here, to my mind at least. Dallas I might have guessed, especially if you factor in South Fork shenanigans. How many marriages can withstand a shower surprise second only to that at the Norman Bates Motel. It's those Russkies who puzzle me. I'd have thought that nothing would breed togetherness like permafrost, but maybe Russian husbands have been practicing glasnost for years.

You Live around Here?

The 10 Worst U.S. Cities
for Finding Single Females

	% Single Women in Female Population
1. Garland, TX	32.1
2. Pasadena, TX	33.6
3. Virginia Beach, VA	34.3
4. Sterling Heights, MI	34.4
5. Chesapeake, VA	35.7
6. Arlington, TX	36.4
7. Anchorage, AK	37.1
7. Mesa, AZ	37.1
9. Casper, WY	37.2
10. Amarillo, TX	37.8

—From *199 American Cities Compared*, Information Publications, Burlington, VT, 1984 (1980 figures).

This suggests that the west is still in need of a good mail-order-bride service. I can well understand why no woman in her right mind would want to venture alone into many of the above cities, but what puzzles me is why any guy would want to either. That's especially true for Virginia Beach, one hell of a threatening wilderness, especially on summer weekends.

Forget Sadie Hawkins Day

The 10 Worst U.S. Cities
for Finding Single Males

	% Single Men in Male Population
1. Garland, TX	28.5
2. Independence, MO	30.0

3. Sterling Heights, MI	31.2
4. Amarillo, TX	31.3
5. Mesa, AZ	32.7
6. Hialeah, FL	33.4
7. Chesapeake, VA	33.4
8. Pasadena, TX	33.7
9. Hollywood, FL	33.8
10. Pierre, SD	34.3

—From *199 American Cities Compared*, Information Publications, Burlington, VT, 1984 (1980 figures).

Turns out there aren't many single guys around these parts either. What is it that is driving everyone to marry? Sales on rice? On dinette sets? I was looking for at least one Utah city here, in which case we might well include married men looking for single women, as is the Mormon tradition, inexplicably largely abandoned.

No Elbow Room

The 10 Worst U.S. Cities in Population Density

	Persons/Sq Mi
1. New York, NY	23,455
2. Jersey City, NJ	16,934
3. Paterson, NJ	16,623
4. San Francisco, CA	14,633
5. Newark, NJ	13,662
6. Chicago, IL	13,174
7. Trenton, NJ	13,161
8. Philadelphia, PA	12,413
9. Boston, MA	11,928
10. Washington, DC	10,181

—From *199 American Cities Compared*, Information Publications, Burlington, VT, 1984 (1980 figures).

Take this another way: Factor in George Steinbrenner, a few Bernard Goetz partisans, and a bunch of Rockefeller Center execs, and you have some very dense people indeed. Nothing to match #10, however.

You Didn't Move for the Schools

The 20 Worst U.S. Metropolitan Areas for Educational Effort and Opportunities*

1. Pascagoula, MS

2. Richland-Kennewick-Pasco, WA

3. Houma-Thibodaux, LA

4. Visalia-Tulare-Porterville, CA

5. Rochester, MN

6. Stockton, CA

7. Oxnard-Ventura, CA

8. Anniston, AL

9. Aurora-Elgin, IL

10. Dothan, AL

11. Las Vegas, NV

12. Huntsville, AL

13. Gadsden, AL

14. Lafayette, LA

15. Vancouver, WA

16. Fayetteville-Springdale, AR

17. Lake Charles, LA

18. San Francisco, CA

19. Salt Lake City-Ogden, UT

20. Columbia, MO

*Criteria used are pupil-teacher ratio in the public school system (K–12), financial effort index, and options in higher education.

—From Richard Boyer and David Savageau, *Places Rated Almanac,* Rand McNally, Chicago, 1985.

The Blackboard Jungle

The 10 U.S. Metropolitan Areas with the Worst Pupil-Teacher Ratios

	Ratio
1. Vancouver, WA	20.52
2. Bremerton, WA	20.30
3. Vallejo-Fairfield-Napa, CA	20.27
4. Jacksonville, NC	20.17
5. Seattle, WA	20.15
6. San Jose, CA	19.83
7. Las Vegas, NV	19.82
8. Richland-Kennewick-Pasco, WA	19.59
9. Provo-Orem, UT	19.54
10. Dothan, AL	19.35

—From U.S. Bureau of the Census and Market Data Retrieval, National School Market Index, 1983.

I Don't Need No Schoolin'

*The 10 U.S. Cities with the Most People
Having Less Than 5 Years* of Schooling*

	% of Population
1. El Paso, TX	11.0
2. Oxnard, CA	10.8
3. San Antonio, TX	10.6
4. Newark, NJ	10.1
5. San Bernardino, CA	9.6
6. Corpus Christi, TX	9.4
7. Santa Ana, CA	9.3
8. Miami, FL	9.0
9. Hartford, CT	8.9
10. Paterson, NJ	8.5

—From *199 American Cities Compared,* Information Publications, Burlington, VT, 1984 (U.S. Census, 1980).

We're Waiting 'til It's a Movie

*The 12 U.S. Metropolitan Areas with the
Worst-Read Citizens**

1. Canton, OH

2. Binghamton, NY

3. Longview-Marshall, TX

4. Fitchburg-Leominster, MA

5. Fort Lauderdale–Hollywood–Pompano Beach, FL

6. Biloxi-Gulfport, MS

7. Harrisburg-Lebanon-Carlisle, PA

7. Williamsport, PA

9. Birmingham, AL

10. Allentown-Bethlehem, PA, NJ

10. Scranton–Wilkes-Barre, PA

10. Wichita Falls, TX

*Criterion used is the number of volumes in area libraries, plus circulation, divided by population.

—From Richard Boyer and David Savageau, *Places Rated Almanac*, Rand McNally, Chicago, 1985.

Shall we contemplate the rammerpercussions of this localized illiteracy? Do they have talking traffic signals? Is there a ban on foreign films with subtitles, or do they play them at half-speed? Is the public library exclusively video rental? Sounds like a Nielsen executive's paradise to me.

Ain't Got No Culture Here

The 20 Worst U.S. Metropolitan Areas for Cultural Facilities*

1. Sharon, PA

2. Texarkana, TX, AR

3. Sherman-Denison, TX

4. Kankakee, IL

5. Benton Harbor, MI

6. Joplin, MO

7. Danville, WA

8. Victoria, TX

9. Fort Walton Beach, FL

10. Parkersburg-Marietta, WV, OH

11. Clarksville-Hopkinsville, TN, KY

12. Dothan, AL

13. Yuba City, CA

14. Burlington, NC

15. Fort Smith, AR, OK

16. Steubenville-Weirton, OH, WV

17. Pascagoula, MS

18. Laredo, TX

19. Gadsden, AL

20. Bradenton, FL

*Criterion used is the number of museums, fine-arts galleries, public radio television stations, universities offering degrees in the arts, symphony orchestras, theaters, opera companies, dance companies, and public libraries.

—From Richard Boyer and David Savageau, *Places Rated Almanac*, Rand McNally, Chicago, 1985.

I Don't Think It's Coming Here

*The 10 Worst U.S. Metropolitan Areas for Access to a Movie Theater**

	Residents/ Theater
1. Utica-Rome, NY	160,090
2. Scranton–Wilkes-Barre, PA	104,114
3. Pittsfield, MA	83,490
4. Lowell, MA, NH	81,407
5. Niagara Falls, NY	75,785
6. Washington, DC, MD, VA	73,882
7. Bristol, CT	73,762
8. Louisville, KY, IN	73,597

9. Lancaster, PA		72,469
10. Chattanooga, TN, GA		71,090

*Criterion used is population divided by number of 4-walled theaters.

—From Richard Boyer and David Savageau, *Places Rated Almanac*, Rand McNally, Chicago, 1985.

How have they suffered in Utica? Do they think Star Wars is a term invented by Reagan? Is Out of Africa merely a sensible career move? Is Porky's just some place not to hold a bar mitzvah? By and large, they are blessed.

Let's Go Watch the Haircuts

*The 20 Worst U.S. Metropolitan Areas for Recreational Opportunities**

1. Gadsden, AL

2. Danville, VA

3. Fitchburg-Leominster, MA

4. Anderson, SC

5. Tyler, TX

6. Texarkana, TX, AR

7. Burlington, NC

8. Laredo, TX

9. Fayetteville, NC

10. Dothan, AL

11. Williamsport, PA

12. Greeley, CO

13. Bristol, CT

14. Pine Bluff, AR

15. Hickory, NC

16. Florence, SC

17. Joplin, M

18. Modesto, CA

19. Longview-Marshall, TX

20. Manchester, NH

*Criterion used is the number of good restaurants; public golf courses; certified tenpin bowling lanes; movie theaters; zoos; aquaria; family theme parks; sanctioned automobile racetracks; pari-mutuel betting attractions; major- and minor-league professional sports teams; NCAA Division I football and basketball teams; miles of ocean or Great Lakes coastline; inland bodies of water; and national forests, parks, and wildlife refuges.

———

—From Richard Boyer and David Savageau, *Places Rated Almanac,* Rand McNally, Chicago, 1985.

At least in the case of #3 these are the very same people who have a hard time reading. No place to go and nothing to do at home but watch the tube. Let's match these with the suicide stats.

Have Niblick, Will Travel

The 10 Worst U.S. Metropolitan Areas for Access to Public Golf Courses

	Residents/Course
1. Anderson, SC	No course
2. Bristol, CT	No course
3. Gadsden, AL	No course
4. Jersey City, NJ	1,113,944
5. Portsmouth-Dover-Rochester, NH, ME	381,876
6. New York, NY	359,781

7. Houma-Thibodaux, LA	353,752
8. Montgomery, AL	272,867
9. Hagerstown, MD	226,172
10. Texarkana, TX, AR	226,134

—From the National Golf Foundation, 1984.

7–10 Split

*The 10 Worst U.S. Metropolitan Areas
for Access to Tenpin Bowling*

	Residents/Lane
1. Boston, MA	16,313
2. Portland, ME	13,845
3. Birmingham, AL	6,596
4. Galveston–Texas City, TX	6,123
5. Jackson, MS	5,839
6. Fresno, CA	5,306
7. Laredo, TX	4,962
8. McAllen-Edinburg- Mission, TX	4,702
9. Springfield, IL	4,694
10. Florence, SC	4,590

—From the American Bowling Congress, 1984.

*And you thought it was an accident I moved to Beantown.
Regrettably, this stat is deceiving, as New England is infested with
an even sillier variant tandem, duckpins and candlepins. The ball
and pins are smaller and they give you more tosses. But no matter how many you take, they are never enough to knock down
the pins and always too many to watch.*

If We Don't Cook, Who Will?

The 17 U.S. Metropolitan Areas with No
Quality Restaurants

Anderson, IN
Anderson, SC
Brazoria, TX
Burlington, NC
Danville, VA
Fitchburg-Leominster, MA
Gadsden, AL
Hamilton-Middletown, OH
Houma-Thibodaux, LA
Jacksonville, AL
Jersey City, NJ
Muncie, IN
Panama City, FL
Texarkana, TX, AR
Tyler, TX
Waterbury, CT
Yakima, WA

—From *Mobil Travel Guide*, Rand McNally, Chicago, 1984.

"Quality restaurants" is the tough nut to swallow here. Mobil's definition may be restaurants not attached to a gas station or restaurants serving food that takes more than 30 seconds to fry. If Michelin were doing the ratings, we'd be talking the entire subcontinent. It is intriguing to note that cities called "Anderson" must specialize in home cooking.

Plenty of Reservations (Part I)

*The 6 Worst Holidays for Eating Out**

	% Adults Who Eat Out
1. Grandparents' Day	5
2. Secretary's Day	6
3. Labor Day	8
4. Christmas	9
5. Memorial Day	10
5. St. Patrick's Day	10

—*The most popular day for eating out is your own birthday—49 percent of American adults do.

Plenty of Reservations (Part II)

*New Restaurant Concepts Americans Are Least Likely to Visit in the Next 3 Months**

	% Say Will Try
1. Sushi	8
2. Gourmet hot dogs	14
2. Mesquite grilling	14
4. Cajun spicy food	15
5. Marinated, broiled, or Mexican chicken	18
5. Diet cuisine	18

*Of 16 different specialties surveyed, summer 1986.

—Both above lists are from the National Restaurant Association.

First off, how many of you, not employed by Hallmark, knew there was a Grandparents' Day? I'm surprised that so many eat out on St. Patrick's Day. Those I've seen ambulatory on that date aren't interested in taking solids. And the thought of eating green anything is not appetizing. That same sentiment obviously holds for raw fish, seaweed, and horseradish, as well it should. If the Japanese wish to consume what we wisely avoid, more power to them. I suspect those who do go to a sushi bar are merely responding in Pavlovian fashion to the word "bar." As for gourmet hot dogs, we're talking oxymoron here, aren't we? Or do such radical gestures as using meat from a domesticated animal or abjuring chemicals best left at toxic dumps make a hot dog a gourmet item? I've known too many trendy people who would eat their shoes if grilled over mesquite or made painfully spicy by Cajun burning. These chickens sound like what's been offered in Manhattan storefronts, and largely shunned, for decades. And who'd pay good money for a meal that isn't filling? At least starving is free. (

Where Are You Glowing?

The 5 U.S. Metropolitan Areas with the Most Nuclear Power Plants

	Plants
1. Charlotte–Gastonia–Rock Hill, NC, SC	4
1. Joliet, IL	4
3. New London–Norwich, CT, RI	3
3. Phoenix, AZ	3
3. San Diego, CA	3

—From Richard Boyer and David Savageau, *Places Rated Almanac*, Rand McNally, Chicago, 1985.

No, Chernobyl is not a sister city to any of these. And no, you can't take your temperature with your finger or read by the light of your nose. Not yet, at least.

Make a Buck, Spend a Buck

The 15 U.S. Metropolitan Areas with the Worst Cost of Living*

		Index†
1.	Stamford, CT	179
2.	Oxnard-Ventura, CA	177
3.	Norwalk, CT	162
4.	Honolulu, HI	158
5.	San Francisco, CA	153
6.	Anchorage, AK	142
7.	San Jose, CA	140
8.	Anaheim–Santa Ana, CA	139
9.	Santa Barbara–Santa Maria–Lompoc, CA	136
10.	Bergen-Passaic, NJ	135
11.	Danbury, CT	133
11.	New York, NY	133
11.	Newark, NJ	133
11.	Oakland, CA	133
15.	Santa Rosa–Petaluma, CA	132

*Criterion used is the cost to a middle-class family of homeownership, food, and other goods and services, rated on an index for which the national average is 100.

†Average =100.

—From Richard Boyer and David Savageau, *Places Rated Almanac*, Rand McNally, Chicago, 1985.

For Hawaii, even Honolulu, it's worth the money; the same for San Francisco. And Anchorage is understandable, when you factor in the cost of air-freighting in anything with vitamins and no blubber. But pay extra to live in Newark? That is truly cruel and unusual punishment.

Get Out to Get Ahead

*The 20 Worst U.S. Metropolitan Areas for Personal Economic Outlook**

1. Eugene-Springfield, OR
2. Beaver County, PA
3. Williamsport, PA
4. Lorain-Elyria, OH
5. Anderson, IN
6. Kokomo, IN
7. Provo-Orem, UT
8. Benton Harbor, MI
9. Medford, OR
10. Muskegon, MI
11. Saginaw–Bay City–Midland, MI
12. Flint, MI
13. Steubenville-Weirton, OH, WV
14. Jackson, MI
15. Gary-Hammond, IN
16. Salem, OR
17. Youngstown-Warren, OH
18. Detroit, MI
19. Duluth, MN, WI
20. Dubuque, IA

*Criteria used are average household income adjusted for taxes and living costs, rate of income growth, and rate of job expansion.

—From Richard Boyer and David Savageau, *Places Rated Almanac,* Rand McNally, Chicago, 1985.

Anderson (#5), you may recall, was also a place without a decent restaurant to its name. Clearly there are no opportunities in food management there. Cordon Bleu graduates are advised to steer clear. Detroit isn't necessarily such a bad place to work—if your name is Jack Morris or Thomas Hearns.

Brother, Can You Spare a Dime?

The 10 Worst U.S. Cities for per Capita Income

		Ave Ann Income, $
1.	Newark, NJ	4,525
2.	Paterson, NJ	5,060
3.	Trenton, NJ	5,400
4.	El Paso, TX	5,439
5.	Hartford, CT	5,559
6.	San Antonio, TX	5,671
7.	Cleveland, OH	5,770
8.	Dayton, OH	5,771
9.	Jersey City, NJ	5,812
10.	Springfield, MA	5,819

—From *199 American Cities Compared,* Information Publications, Burlington, VT, 1984 (U.S. Census, 1980).

Can Your Wife Spare a Dime?

The 10 Worst U.S. Cities for Household Income

		Ave Ann Income, $
1.	Newark, NJ	10,118
2.	Miami, FL	11,097
3.	Atlanta, GA	11,297
4.	Providence, RI	11,437

5. St. Louis, MO	11,511
6. Hartford, CT	11,513
7. Buffalo, NY	11,593
8. New Haven, CT	11,683
9. Wilmington, DE	11,695
10. Tallahassee, FL	11,750

—From *199 American Cities Compared*, Information Publications, Burlington, VT, 1984 (U.S. Census, 1980).

If this seems like far too little money to support a house or the people in it, just be grateful, as these folks must be, that the government has succeeded in eliminating poverty to the extent that we can safely reduce welfare spending by a large percentage without adversely affecting electoral results.

My House Is the Bank's House

The 20 U.S. Metropolitan Areas with the Worst Homeowners' Bills*

	Ave Ann Bills, $
1. Stamford, CT	23,640
2. Norwalk, CT	20,151
3. San Francisco, CA	17,158
4. Honolulu, HI	17,021
5. San Jose, CA	16,048
6. Anaheim–Santa Ana, CA	16,047
7. Santa Barbara–Santa Maria–Lompoc, CA	15,547
8. Bergen-Passaic, NJ	14,607
9. San Diego, CA	14,465
10. Danbury, CT	14,420
11. Santa Cruz, CA	14,303
12. Newark, NJ	14,220
13. Oxnard-Ventura, CA	14,000

14. Los Angeles–Long Beach, CA	13,868
15. Salinas-Seaside-Monterey, CA	13,838
16. Washington, DC, MD, VA	13,724
17. Bridgeport-Milford, CT	13,429
18. New York, NY	13,358
19. Lake County, IL	13,282
20. Oakland, CA	13,135

*Combined utility bills, property taxes, and mortgage payments.

—From Richard Boyer and David Savageau, *Places Rated Almanac*, Rand McNally, Chicago, 1985.

These numbers are all startling, but consider #12 a moment. This is the same city where per capita income was the nation's lowest, $4525 a year, the year before this study was made. Unless they've got at least 4 average earners to a pad in Newark, they can't afford to keep the house, let alone pay for food, clothing, and other frivolities.

I'm Gonna Kill My Landlord

The 13 U.S. Metropolitan Areas with the Worst Monthly Rent

	Ave Mo Rent, $
1. Anchorage, AK	520
2. Anaheim–Santa Ana, CA	510
3. Reno, NV	490
4. San Jose, CA	480
4. Stamford, CT	480
6. Nassau-Suffolk, NY	475
7. Norwalk, CT	465

8. Middlesex-Somerset-	
Hunterdon, NJ	455
9. Casper, WY	445
10. Las Vegas, NV	430
11. Bergen-Passaic, NJ	415
12. Richland-Kennewick-	
Pasco, WA	410
13. Seattle, WA	400

—From Richard Boyer and David Savageau, *Places Rated Almanac*, Rand McNally, Chicago, 1985.

My House Is the City's House

The 10 U.S. Metropolitan Areas with the Worst Property Tax

	Ave Ann Tax, $
1. Stamford, CT	3061
2. Bergen-Passaic, NJ	2777
3. Newark, NJ	2695
4. Norwalk, CT	2576
5. New York, NY	2562
6. Middlesex-Somerset-	
Hunterdon, NJ	2553
6. Monmouth-Ocean	
Counties, NJ	2553
8. Ann Arbor, MI	2132
9. Salem-Gloucester, MA	2066
10. Danbury, CT	1779

—From Richard Boyer and David Savageau, *Places Rated Almanac*, Rand McNally, Chicago, 1985.

Tax Revolting

The 10 States with the Worst
Cumulative Tax Burden per Capita*

		Ave Ann Tax, $
1.	Hawaii	982
2.	New York	788
3.	California	691
4.	Maryland	662
5.	Wyoming	622
6.	Wisconsin	611
7.	Minnesota	605
8.	Virginia	575
9.	Massachusetts	565
10.	New Mexico	556

*Taxes included are personal income tax, general sales tax, gasoline tax, driver's license fees, and automobile registration fees.

—From *Tax Capacity of the Fifty States*, Advisory Commission on Intergovernmental Relations, 1983.

My House Is Your House

The 9 Worst U.S. Metropolitan Areas
in Percentage of Single-Family Dwellings

		% Housing
1.	Jersey City, NJ	12
2.	New York, NY	17
3.	Boston, MA	22
4.	Lewiston-Auburn, ME	41
5.	Chicago, IL	46
5.	Lawrence-Haverhill, MA, NH	46
7.	Anchorage, AK	48
7.	Fall River, MA, RI	48

9. Fort Lauderdale–Hollywood–Pompano Beach, FL	50
9. Honolulu, HI	50
9. Miami-Hialeah, FL	50

—From Richard Boyer and David Savageau, *Places Rated Almanac*, Rand McNally, Chicago, 1985.

I believe this factor is thought of by some as an indicator of density, high real estate prices, and poor economic means. Yet it could just as easily indicate a spirit of camaraderie that would permit any of the above to supplant Philadelphia as the City of Brotherly Love. Cambodian refugees share overpriced rentals because they want to? Then ketchup is a vegetable.

An Arm and a Leg for a Suit

The 10 Most Expensive Cities on Earth for Buying Men's Clothes

	$*
1. Manama	596
2. Jidda	548
3. New York	492
4. Chicago	490
5. Tokyo	486
6. Copenhagen	467
7. Montreal	466
8. Los Angeles	462
9. San Francisco	460
10. Buenos Aires	455

*Figure includes the cost of a 2-piece ready-to-wear suit, blazer, shirt, pair of socks, and shoes in a department store, 1982–1983.

—From John T. Marlin, Immanuel Ness, and Stephen T. Collins, *Book of World City Rankings*, Free Press, New York, 1986.

Don't ask me where Manama is. All I know is if I ever go there I plan to dress down. The same goes for my wife.

Putting the Haute in Haute Couture

The 10 Most Expensive Cities on Earth for Buying Women's Clothes

		$*
1.	Buenos Aires	449
2.	Tokyo	432
3.	Chicago	394
4.	Jidda	369
5.	New York	334
6.	Copenhagen	312
7.	Oslo	308
8.	San Francisco	300
9.	Munich	297
10.	Manama	296

*Figure includes the cost of a summer dress, blazer, skirt, pair of tights, and fashionable day shoes in a department store, in 1982.

—From John T. Marlin, Immanuel Ness, and Stephen T. Collins, *Book of World City Rankings*, Free Press, New York, 1986.

Give Us Now Our Daily Crumb

The 11 Most Expensive Major Cities on Earth for Buying a Loaf of Bread

		$
1.	Munich	1.84
2.	Frankfurt	1.74
3.	Sapporo	1.68

4. Düsseldorf	1.66
5. Osaka	1.55
6. Yokohama	1.49
7. Kobe	1.45
8. Nagoya	1.43
9. Tokyo	1.40
10. Kyoto	1.34
10. Vancouver	1.34

*Rated between 1979–1983.

—From John T. Marlin, Immanuel Ness, and Stephen T. Collins, *Book of World City Rankings*, Free Press, New York, 1986.

I associated Japanese starch consumption with rice, not bread. Now I know why.

I'll Gladly Pay You Tuesday for a Hamburger Today

*The 10 Most Expensive Major Cities on Earth for Buying a Pound of Meat**

	$/lb, Ave
1. Kobe	4.90
2. Sapporo	4.77
3. Nagoya	4.60
4. Tokyo	4.54
5. Kyoto	4.40
6. Seoul	4.32
7. Yokohama	4.27
8. Osaka	4.00
9. Düsseldorf	3.42
10. Paris	3.00

*Beef, chicken, and pork, rated 1982–1983.

—From John T. Marlin, Immanuel Ness, and Stephen T. Collins, *Book of World City Rankings*, Free Press, New York, 1986.

If they have Wendy's in Kobe, which I hope for their sake (read either way) they don't, does it have a loan manager? A couple of Big Classics could mean a second mortgage.

They're Too High in Cholesterol Anyway

The 12 Most Expensive Major Cities on Earth for Buying a Dozen Eggs*

	$
1. Melbourne	1.64
2. Brisbane	1.51
3. Sydney	1.49
4. London	1.48
5. Munich	1.44
6. Edinburgh	1.40
6. Glasgow	1.40
6. Perth	1.40
9. Birmingham	1.38
9. Leeds	1.38
9. Liverpool	1.38
9. Manchester	1.38

*Rated between 1979–1983.

—From John T. Marlin, Immanuel Ness, and Stephen T. Collins, *Book of World City Rankings*, Free Press, New York, 1986.

Australia is clearly not the place to order a soufflé. Did they kill off the chickens when they wiped out the rabbits? Or are they waiting for duckbill platypuses to lay some eggs?

Forget the Microwave

The 10 Most Expensive Major Cities on Earth for Buying Household Appliances

	$*
1. Bogotá	3944
2. Bangkok	3530
3. Bombay	3275
4. Seoul	3024
5. Manama	2905
6. Jakarta	2856
7. Athens	2855
8. Zurich	2580
9. Montreal	2573
10. Tel Aviv	2518

*Buys electric or gas 3- or 4-burner range, refrigerator/freezer, electric sewing machine, 22-inch color television set, canister vacuum cleaner, and steam iron; rated 1982–1983.

—From John T. Marlin, Immanuel Ness, and Stephen T. Collins, *Book of World City Rankings*, Free Press, New York, 1986.

Consider, however, that you don't need a stove to cook things in many of these locations; you can fry eggs on the sidewalk. Nor do you need an iron. And unless you like watching dubbed Happy Days reruns and presidential proclamations, there isn't much on the tube either.

When You've Got a Lemon Make a Car

*The 8 Worst Cars, According to Their Owners**

1. Yugo	2359
2. Alfa Romeo	209

3.	AMC/Jeep/Renault	103
4.	Peugeot	93
5.	Porsche	76
6.	Mitsubishi	73
7.	GM	19
8.	Ford	8

*Number of complaints against manufacturer compared with market share; survey conducted in Massachusetts in 1986 through the state's "lemon-law" arbitration program.

I'm not surprised by #1; the Serbo-Croatian auto industry is not exactly legendary. But where are the British cars? I've driven Lelands, Rovers, Morris Minors, Austin-Healeys, and Triumphs, and have never failed to be impressed by the number, variety, and complexity of the self-inflicted wounds they sustain. Perhaps this fact is so well known that there are no owners around anymore to complain. Or maybe they are just too embarrassed to sound off. That should hold for Yugo owners too.

Wouldn't You Really Rather Have a Buick?

*The 10 Most Unsatisfactory Cars, According to Their Owners**

1. Peugeot

2. AMC/Renault

3. Dodge

4. Isuzu

5. Alfa Romeo

6. Pontiac

7. Plymouth

8. Ford

9. Chrysler

10. Chevrolet

*Based on a 1985 survey of owners of new cars from 29 international makers, conducted 12 to 14 months after purchase.

—From J. D. Power & Associates.

Fill 'er Up, I'm Going Next Door

The 10 Worst Cars for Mileage, 1986 Models

	City/ Highway mpg
1. Rolls-Royce Silver Spur limousine	8/10
2. Rolls-Royce Camargue	8/11
2. Rolls-Royce Corniche II-Continental	8/11
4. Rolls-Royce Silver Spirit-Spur-Mulsanne	9/10
5. Jaguar XJ-S	13/17
6. Mercedes-Benz 560SEC	14/16
6. Mercedes-Benz 560SEL	14/16
8. Mercedes-Benz 560SL	14/17
9. Mercedes-Benz 420SEL	15/18
10. Jaguar XJ 6	15/19

—From EPA ratings.

What's a dollar a gallon, of course, when you've already shelled out $100,000? And who's paying that much anyway? For starters, the Kuwaitis who own most of these cars get their gas pumped with an OPEC card. Or they pump their own.

Hot Wheels

*The 10 Cars Most Often Stolen or Vandalized, 1987 Models**

1. Volkswagen GT1
2. Volkswagen Cabriolet
3. Volkswagen Gulf, 2-door
4. Volkswagen Jetta, 2-door
5. Volkswagen Gulf, 4-door
6. Saab 900, 2-door
7. Cadillac DeVille, 2-door
8. Cadillac Brougham
9. Hyundai Excel
10. Cadillac DeVille, 4-door

*These are cars with the highest claim frequencies, including theft of items from hubcaps to radios to the car itself.

———

—From the Highway Loss Data.

This is indeed puzzling. VWs? The first five are ripped off at least 5 times on average, mostly for radios. I suspect there is an international car ring that has it in for the German auto industry. Radios are the only way to explain the popularity of #9 among heisters, save a death wish.

Great Snorting Road Hogs

The 5 Most Annoying Driving Habits

1. THE AUTOMATIC MERGE—Drivers entering the highway from an access lane invariably, and unaccountably, assume they needn't look to see if there is traffic on the road. Somehow, magically, room will be made for them if they sim-

ply merge blindly into the right-hand lane. For most, this works. The rest will never know what hit them.

2. THE YELLOW LIGHT BURST—Yellow to most drivers means hit the accelerator, so that if they do get sideswiped by a light-jumper from the intersecting street (see #3), it will be at maximum possible impact speed.

3. DRAG-STRIP GREEN LIGHT—This is the driver who, when the light turns green, or a fraction of a second before, hits the accelerator hard. When the wheels stop spinning, the driver may be in orbit. This is, for some strange reason, linked to adolescent male hormonal output.

4. DISASTER WATCHING—The best way to become part of a car wreck is to slow down from highway speed to 5 miles per hour in order to get a closer look at someone else's carnage. Yet the urge is irresistible. Despite their name, rubberneckers are prone to whiplash.

5. TOLL-BOOTH KIBBITZING—The only thing worse than ignoring the human being who takes your money is spending the morning talking with him or her while two dozen horn-blowers wait to get to the office.

Thou Shalt Not Do Any of This Stuff

The 25 Worst Sins, According to Readers of People *Magazine (on a scale of 1 to 10)**

1. Murder	9.84
2. Rape	9.77
3. Incest	9.68
4. Child abuse	9.59
5. Spying against your country	8.98
6. Drug dealing	8.83
7. Embezzlement	8.49
8. Pederasty	8.30
9. Spouse swapping	8.09

10. Adultery	7.63
11. Industrial spying	7.53
12. Bigotry	7.42
13. Suicide	7.31
14. Not helping someone in danger	7.09
15. Sexual harassment	6.97
16. Misrepresenting something you're selling	6.80
17. Taking drugs	6.24
18. Hypocrisy	6.19
19. Atheism	6.12
20. Homosexuality	5.78
21. Abortion	5.77
22. Revenge	5.74
23. Parking in handicapped zone	5.53
24. Killing to protect your property	5.47
25. Greed	5.43

*Based on 1000 responses, chosen randomly, to a poll asking readers to rate 51 activities according to how guilty they would feel if they engaged in that activity and how they would rank it on a morality index.

—From *People*, February 10, 1986.

Remarkable statistics here—especially that murder over possessions is less onerous than parking in a no-parking zone. Does this mean we should give the chair to those who flagrantly jaypark, or $25 tickets to killers? Bear in mind, however, this is people who read People talking.

Go and Sin No More

The Worst Sins, According to Specific Religious Denominations

No one, short of Tom Lehrer, seems to want to make fun of religion. But we do. According to the Society for Promoting Religious Intolerance, which we formed Thursday in Providence,

RI, *here are the worst sins, as ranked by practitioners of the world's leading religions.*

CATHOLICS

1. Having sex without risking unwanted pregnancy
2. Failing to acknowledge as God's emissary on earth a middle-aged Polish skier living in Rome and wearing a beanie
3. Dropping cookies in church
4. Having fun

JEWS

1. Buying retail
2. Eating pork or shellfish when you could be consuming healthful foods like nitrate-cured salmon (lox), cow intestines (stuffed derma), or schmaltz (chicken fat)
3. Not buying Israeli bonds
4. Not writing or calling your mother
5. Having fun

MOSLEMS

1. Buying Israeli bonds
2. Eating pork when you could be consuming healthful foods like camel burgers and fly-covered custard pastries left out in the desert sun
3. Selling rugs wholesale
4. Bypassing Mecca to avoid the downtown traffic
5. Having fun

BAHA'I

1. Misspelling the name of the religion
2. Not explaining your religion to everyone you meet

PROTESTANTS

1. Having fun

Bad Libs

The Unicorn Hunters' Dishonor List of Words and Phrases

1. "The patient did not fulfill his wellness potential." This phrasing obscures the fact that the patient died and "places the blame squarely on the patient," Emmet Donnelly of Detroit notes.

2. "Clients," when speaking of patients.

3. "Neonatal unit," when speaking of a nursery.

4. "You can't take nothing with you." (Credit the late Mayor Harold Washington of Chicago with this one.) Denise Brummel of Hammond, IN, points out that "This is a double negative even if uttered by a mayor whose predecessors found investigations 'fruitworthy' and disliked 'insinuendos.'"

5. "In his own words." Saul Jacobson of Regina, Saskatchewan, asks, "How else would he say it?"

6. "I'm talkin' baseball here." Charlotte Head of Napanee, Ontario, adds, "We're talkin' grammar here."

7. "Shower activity," when speaking of rain.

8. "Partly sunny," Daryl Huggard of Bay City, MI, points out, could refer to a solar eclipse.

9. "Preventatative maintenance" is the U.S. Army's term for "preventive maintenance" and is the winner of the Military Word Prolongation Award.

10. "Turned up missing," which gives a rather mixed message.

11. "Hands-on participatory experience," which says it all, twice.

12. "Colorization." A Unicorn Hunter observes, "It's bad enough that Ted Turner damages classic film. His disrespect for the language is equally reprehensible. He is simply coloring films."

—From wire service reports of the Unicorn Hunters' Eleventh Annual New Year's Dishonor List.

If you haven't heard enough of these phrases for your liking, give Al Haig a call. He's reading this. And taking notes.

ENTERTAINMENT AND CELEBRITY WORSTS

The Greeks had Athena and Ares. We have Vanna White and Tom Cruise. That is the cultural answer to the musical question, "How low can you go?" If we aren't in intellectual limbo, we are at least under the limbo stick.

This society puts much effort into hoisting leaden characters onto pedestals, so who are we to try and knock them off?

Good question, and a rude one. As the Gestapo used to say, *we* will ask the questions. What we wanted to know was who does Frank Deford, who wrote a worthy book on a worthless pageant, think are the worst Miss Americas?

Deford is among the experts who told us which were the worst films, popular songs, television shows, authors, and books in recent memory (theirs, if blissfully no longer ours).

And you the people chose your unfunniest comedians and your most colorless sportscasters on color TV. If the network executives are listening, they can at least take comfort that we are still watching. Various magazines and societies with nothing better to do or print provided lists of the most boring celebrities—the most overrated, overbearing, and overpublicized. May the next thing that is over about them be their careers.

Hell hath no fury like an audience scorned. Or a producer, for that matter. Even pets and children are not exempt from our scrutiny. David Attenborough, celebrant of all life on earth, confessed the 5 animals which most irritated him on location. Elizabeth Taylor was not on his list, perhaps only because they haven't worked together. (They may when he gets around to documenting primitive mating behavior.)

The ill-starred stars cited here will probably complain, possibly sue. You'd think they wouldn't have time to peruse such ephemera as these lists, but consider how often *National Enquirer* and its ilk have found themselves in Perry Masonville. Of course, it is for just such frivolities that celebrities keep press agents, lawyers, and half of the rest of Los Angeles and its near-human types on retainer. (We doubt, however, that we'll hear any flak from three-toed sloths.) But these guys have already had their chance, as far as we're concerned. We wrote to Mickey Rooney asking for his worst marriages, Lucille Ball for her worst falls, Jean Harris for her worst diets, Arnold Schwarzenegger for his worst performances. Yes, it is hard to choose, and we didn't hear from any of them.

A special note to celebrities: It is part of the price of celebrity that you will show up on other people's lists, particularly lists of worsts. And especially if your name is Sylvester Stallone. It often seems as if celebrity is a formula of less-than-Einsteinian sophistication: The louder and less talented you are, the more famous you will become. Hence Stallone. And the corollary: The more famous you make yourself, the more you will complain about it. Hence Madonna and Gary Hart. Not together, that is. I think. But the *Miami Herald* is working on it.

The trivialization of American culture deserves at least another paragraph, but we gotta go now. My publisher's on the line saying I've got to take a lunch with some Beverly Hills flak who's threatening a lawsuit. Something about insulting his client.

Take This Joke, Please

Henny Youngman's 7 Worst Jokes

1. My wife and I always hold hands. If I let go, she shops.

2. My son is a lifeguard...at a carwash.

3. My son is a cmonbak. He stands in back of trucks and yells, "C'mon back."

4. I take my wife everywhere. But she always finds her way home.

5. I told my wife to only buy things marked down. Yesterday she brought home an escalator.

6. Man goes to a psychiatrist. Psychiatrist says, "You're crazy." Man says he wants a second opinion. Psychiatrist says, "All right, you're ugly."

These are classics; no jokes are corny, but call them bad jokes if you want. Then you've got to include my trademark:

7. Take my wife. Please.

———

—Special to *The Worst of Everything* from Henny Youngman.

Up, Down, Around, and Out

The World's Roughest Roller Coasters, According to Paul Ruben

IN HISTORY

THE CRYSTAL BEACH CYCLONE, BUFFALO, NY—Replaced in 1946, this ride was once the most terrifying of all roller-coaster rides. A nurse was kept on duty at all times. The first drop on the ride featured an 85 percent turn to the right that caused patrons to lose hats, coats, teeth, and wigs, and to career into each other, in some cases cracking ribs. In its 20 years of existence there was only one fatality, however—in 1943. A man stood up to remove his suit jacket as the coaster started. His arms locked, and he couldn't sit back down. He was thrown from the car and run over. His heirs sued, claiming the lap bar didn't hold him. The judge put a dog in the coaster to test it, the dog emerged healthy and happy, and the suit was denied. Turns out, the dog, a British bulldog, belonged to the park's maintenance supervisor and rode the coaster daily.

IN OPERATION

RIVERSIDE CYCLONE, AGAWAM, MA—A wooden coaster built by William Cobb of Dallas in 1982, this is the most terrifying of all roller-coaster rides. I was thrown out of my seat 9 times in one ride. Only the lap bar kept me on the ride. You feel like the seat is being pulled out from under you and you are hanging on by your toes. I dearly love it.

———

—Special to *The Worst of Everything* from Paul Ruben, editor of *Rollercoaster* and officer of the American Coaster Enthusiasts.

I know many kind folks like Ruben who adore them, but the only good roller coaster in my book (not this one) is a dead roller coaster. Since waves in the tub make me nauseous and a ride on the teeter-totter has been known to send my lunch into orbit, I can imagine no worse torture than spending 5 minutes in an uncontrolled fall, or hurtling over bumps and curves at g forces only Chuck Yaeger would smile about... unless it's paying money for the privilege and risking having myself made into the Venus de Milo if I stick an appendage out to signal my panic. One could stand up, of course, but it is better to quit while... you know the rest.

Wouldn't You Really Rather Have a Raggedy Ann?

The 6 Worst Children's Toys, According to Peggy Charren

RAMBO—Because it turns a terrorist outlaw into a children's hero

G. I. JOE—Because it glorifies the defense budget

HULK HOGAN, CHUCK NORRIS, AND MR. T—Because they are based on men who substitute brawn for brains

STRAWBERRY SHORTCAKE—Because she and her "berry" strange friends smell funny

---

—Special to *The Worst of Everything* from Peggy Charren, president of Action for Children's Television.

We might well have included the Bradley tank, MX missile, and other outrageously costly, poorly designed, and indiscriminately lethal playthings on former Defense Secretary Cap Weinberger's annual list for Santa. So how come we gave him everything he wanted, to the 50 cents on our tax dollar? Who can say no to a child at Christmas?

Six Feet under the Christmas Tree

The Worst Toys of 1987, According to the ADA

TOYS THAT ARE CHOKING HAZARDS

Tub Doodler #5301
Colorforms Color Change-O-Bath Buddies #1605
Fun Sponge
Bath Chums

TOYS WITH STRONG PROJECTILE FORCE

Zebra Automatic Pistol #770
Gotcha! Gun

TOYS THAT ARE UNSTABLE

The Graduate Booster Seat

FLAMMABLE TOYS

Pillow People Slumber Bag
Mickey Mouse Clubhouse
Fisher-Price Pop-Up Playhouse
Walt Disney's Mickey Snug-Ums
Coke Slumber Bag

TOYS THAT ENCOURAGE IRRESPONSIBLE BEHAVIOR

Tub Alarm Guard

TOYS WITH THROWAWAY DANGER LABELS

Slime Balls
Lite-Up Monster Head Toy

TOYS WITH POOR LABELING: INAPPROPRIATE FOR AGE CITED; MISLEADING

My Dolly's Bottle Feeding Set #88
My Dolly's Delux Mealtime Set
"Little Mommy" Easy Flow Doll Bottle #1015
Downhill Teddy

Gotcha! Gun
Mr. Spudhead
Farm Animals
Paint Set
Go Fly a Kite—Flutterbye

A good list, I'm sure, and an ADA Christmas tradition. But consider the source. Do you want some liberals (spit out the word, Zeke) telling you what toys not to buy? They'd probably rather see us with some "educational" piece of overpriced pink china that was made in Bulgaria and will turn our kids into sissies—or give 'em funny ideas about making things instead of destroying them.

Give Me a 4-Letter Word for Boring

The 20 Worst Crossword-Puzzle Words, According to Eugene Maleska

1. ANOA—Small buffalo of Celebes and the Philippines

2. ESNE—Member of the lowest class, a laborer

3. OGEE—Double curve with the shape of an elongated S

4. ORAD—Toward the mouth

5. ITER—Canal or passage (anatomical)

6. ALAR—Of or pertaining to wings

7. EMIR—Arabian prince or chieftain

8. OMAR—Boy's name

9. ULE—(suffix) Small-sized

10. EMU—Electromagnetic unit or large, flightless Australian bird

11. ERNE OR ERN—Any of several old world sea eagles

12. ANI—Chiefly tropical American bird with black plumage and long tail

13. ITEA—Genus of shrubs with small white flowers

14. OCA—South American wood sorrel

15. ETUI—Case for holding small articles such as toiletries

16. ENOS—Son of Seth

17. ESTE—Italian family, rulers of Ferrara (1209–1598)

18. ERST—At first, formerly (archaic)

19. ERME—Grieve

20. MOA—Extinct, long-necked, flightless birds of New Zealand

---

—Special to *The Worst of Everything* from Eugene Maleska, crossword editor of the *New York Times.*

Widely said to be a kind and courteous man, Mr. Maleska has become himself a 7-letter word for torture for those of us who attempt the Times crossword. I do mine in ink and write the same letter in every box. I've never failed to finish and to impress those who don't get too close to my paper on the train. The results might cause Mr. Maleska to erme, but what choice do we esnes have?

That Was the Year That Wasn't (Part I)

The Worst of 1986, According to Us *Magazine*

WORST SONG—*"Rock Me Amadeus"* by *Falco*. "Rock me to sleep, maybe. This is one for Puttin' on the Misses."

WORST PERFORMANCE DIRECTED BY A FAMILY MEMBER —*Nicolas Cage*. "You know there's something wrong when all you notice about an actor's performance is that his voice and hair color change in every scene. You were great in *Birdy* and *Valley Girl*, but what were you up to in *Peggy Sue Got Married?* And why didn't your uncle, director Francis Coppola, reel you in? Isn't nepotism supposed to give you a chance to show what you can do?"

WORST MOVIE—*Cobra*. "So this is what *Beverly Hills Cop* would have been like if Sly Stallone had gone ahead with it. But he left, taking this monosyllabic script. By Italian Stallone standards, *Cobra* was flaccid at the box office. No matter. There's always his new ten-picture deal. Crime *is* a disease, Sly, but next time, cure it in private."

WORST MAKEOVER—*Michael Jackson*

WORST INVENTION—*Cerebrex*. "Tired? Run down? You need Cerebrex. Its Japanese inventor swears one hour's snooze ($20) in his comfy chair is as good as eight hours' sleep in a bed. But could you doze off with your head in…a pod?"

WORST SITCOM—*Night Court*. "Even Harry Anderson, Markie Post and Richard Moll can't save this mistrial. Tasteless jokes and mawkish plots do not a good sitcom make. *Night Court* spoils NBC's superb Thursday. It oughta be adjourned."

WORST ONE-SHOT DRAMATIC PERFORMANCE—*Mare Winningham*, in *Who is Julia?* "We love you, Mare, but whatever possessed you to do a TV movie about a brain transplant? Intoned one doctor, 'We may be reaching too high.' Or too low."

WORST ON-SCREEN CHEMISTRY—*(1) Robert Redford* and *Darryl Hannah, (2) Judd Nelson* and *Ally Sheedy, (3) Paul Hogan* and *Linda Kozlowski*. "No worries, mate? Sure *Crocodile Dundee* was a sleeper smash, but those scenes between Hogan and Kozlowski were hardly spontaneous combustion. Nor did we notice a single spark between Hannah and Redford in *Legal Eagles*. But the year's worst matchup has to be Judd 'n Ally in the stupefying *Blue City*. Wasn't it enough they doused *St. Elmo's Fire?*"

WORST PARTY—*The MTV Awards*. "The working press hated this year's multivenue MTV awards. New York scribes were stuck in a wind-whipped tent outside the Palladium. Inside it was hard to see the stage, and the celebrity octane was low. (Look, sis! It's the Hooters!) C'mon, guys, we expect better from you."

WORST GAFFE—*Sondra Gottlieb*. "It was the slap heard 'round the world. Frazzled before a dinner for her prime minister, Gottlieb, wife of Canada's ambassador, publicly struck her social secretary. Since then, the Embassy's entertainment budget has been cut by $30,000. Explained an official, 'It was part of a general reduction...to all Canadian heads of mission.'"

WORST VILLAINS—*Muammar Qaddafi, Abu Nidal, and Kurt Waldheim*.

WORST SOAP PLOT TWIST—*The Dallas Dream*. "'You mostly hear from people who are unhappy about it,' says executive producer Leonard Katzman. That means *US!*"

WORST CAREER MOVIE—*Clint Eastwood*. "Not everyone loves this Carmel topping. Local bumper stickers gripe, Save Carmel—Impeach Clint. Legalizing ice cream cones? We'd rather see you on screen more often."

—From *Us*, December 29, 1986.

Us *leaves the picking in 1987 to its readers, with results in the February 22, 1988, issue. Alas, we went to press before then. So here's to remembering a year that is by now well forgotten. Ditto, the next two lists.*

That Was the Year That Wasn't (Part II)

The Most Mediocre Events and People of 1986,
According to the Millard Fillmore Society

HALLEY'S COMET—All fluff and glitter with no substance

RUNNERS-UP

Joan Rivers (missing the glitter but still all fluff with no substance)
Herb of the Burger King advertisements
Max Headroom
Vanna White

—Awarded by the Society for the Preservation and Enhancement of the Recognition of Millard Fillmore, the last of the Whigs.

Who am I to call the kettle black? But just what the hell is the Millard Fillmore Society anyway? This is no doubt a well-intended and highly motivated organization, like the International Dull Folks Unlimited (see below), but most of these organizations are the work of some press agent, created for the sake of the year-ending UPI and AP fillers they work their way into, never to be heard from again. These guys seem to have confused mediocrity with meaninglessness.

Ho Hum Along with Letterman

The 7 Dullest People of 1986, According
to International Dull Folks Unlimited

1. DAVID LETTERMAN—"A TV host who can't get on the air until after midnight and whose shtick is a stupid pet trick."

2. SAM WALTON—The Arkansas millionaire retail-chain founder "drives an old red-and-white pickup and stands in line in his own Wal-Mart stores."

3. ANN LANDERS.

4. Tom Brokaw.

5. Pee-Wee Herman.

6. Aaron Spelling.

7 Beetle Bailey.

—From J. D. Stewart, chairman of the bored, International Dull Folks Unlimited.

Are You Still Up?

The Most Boring Celebrities of 1987

Jim and Tammy Bakker

HONOR ROLL

Vanna White
Oliver North
Moonlighting
The British Royal Family
Donna Rice
Oral Roberts
John McEnroe
Max Headroom
Sean Penn and Madonna

—Selected by the Boring Institute.

All News That Fits We Print

The 9 Worst Media Excesses of the 1980s, According to Charles Paul Freund

1. The Teflon President—Reagan, throughout most of his presidency, has been not only unchallenged but celebrated by a press corps that has bought into "feel-good" mania. Reagan's popularity is personal, not political, as the Senate elections of 1986 demonstrated.

2. **THE GREAT PATRIOTIC REVIVAL**—High national morale is better than malaise, but the breathless exploitation of the 1984 Olympics, the Statue of Liberty Centennial, etc., has cheapened patriotism and its symbols.

3. **AMERICAN HELD HOSTAGE**—A genuine issue—terrorism—has been reduced to soap opera through exploitation of family members and "human-interest" angles.

4. **RAMBO AS CULTURAL METAPHOR**—The lazy application of a popular movie character to a nation's apparently militaristic frame of mind has completely missed the truth. Americans' support of military action is both cautious and grim: They view it as an unhappy necessity. Gary Cooper in *High Noon* would be a better metaphor.

5. **MUAMMAR QADDAFI'S THREAT TO THE WESTERN WORLD**—However loose a cannon Qaddafi may be, more terrorist incidents seem to have been directed *against* Libya than are attributable to that nation.

6. **SELFISH YUPPIES**—They exist, but concentration on them as a social phenomenon of the 1980s reflects pop sociology. As soon as Yuppieism stopped selling papers, a mother lode of "compassionate" and "socially committed" young professionals was located.

7. **THE DRUG BUBBLE OF 1986**—Nancy Reagan's overblown cause. All perspective on a real-enough problem was lost: Drug use had, in fact, been decreasing all along.

8. **THE DANGER OF VIDEO GAMES**—Supposed to leave young players penniless and addicted, these games have proved as addictive as coonskin caps.

9. **THE ELECTRONIC FUTURE**—PCs were supposed to rewire Americans' personal lives. In fact, few at-home applications have panned out. The same was expected for the new world of TV, though all that Americans have wanted from the box is to continue watching it.

—Special to *The Worst of Everything* from Charles Paul Freund, a regular contributor to the *New Republic*.

That nothing succeeds like excess is a lesson not lost on the American media. But I think we've had too little, not too much of one big-ticket item: Iranscam. Everyone, media included, seems to think we're accustomed to law-skirting and prevaricating presidents, and so we let Ronnie off the hook without clarion calls for impeachment or even gavel-to-gavel TV of the hearings. Have we and the media become so corrupted or jaded ourselves that we can't throw stones of outrage anymore?

Creature Features

Marian Christy's 5 Worst Celebrity Interviews

1. ANDY WARHOL—Funny but impossible. We met for lunch at the Plaza Hotel in New York. He brought with him a woman who never said a word but who was obviously auditing the interview. I asked questions and Warhol gave answers that had no apparent relation to the questions. Example: "Why did you paint the Campbell Soup can?" Answer: "The American flag is red-white-blue."

2. DIANA VREELAND—She looked like a cigar-store Indian, always wore red to her all-red office (that featured touches of leopard and tiger prints), burned incense at noon, and despised fledglings (which I was at the time). I asked her why *Vogue*, the fashion magazine she edited, was running pieces on topless African tribeswomen. Without hesitation, she threw me out of her office.

3. HERMIONE GINGOLD—A most unpleasant meeting, so much so that I had to leave, told her so, but I also asked why she had behaved so badly. She explained her rudeness with "I hate green," looking hard at my green dress. I told her to ignore the green, and began the interview again. When it was over, she said, "I'm sorry." The tone was sweet, too sweet. "But it was all your fault," she said.

4. MAMA GABOR—A frustrated actress who needed an audience, a stage. I became the focus of a dramatic scene.

She had a tantrum at the Plaza, saying she was used to being picked up by limousines, not taxis, and that I should have sent a chauffeur to transport her from her apartment a few blocks away. I let her rant and rave while the crowd gathered. When I could get a word in edgewise, I offered to buy her a cup of coffee, which offer she accepted.

5. GLORIA SWANSON—She had just written a book in which she included Joseph Kennedy among her lovers. I had to talk to her about the affair because it was news. I explained that to her and spoke gently. She screamed, stomped her foot, refused to continue, and pointed to the door. I distracted her by quoting the details of the Kennedy romance.

—Special to *The Worst of Everything* from Marian Christy, nationally syndicated celebrity interviewer of the *Boston Globe*.

You think investigative reporters have it tough? Imagine having to interview the likes of these for a living. That most are no longer living does not make the job any easier.

There She Goes, Good Riddance!

The 5 Worst Miss Americas, According to Frank Deford

1. VANESSA WILLIAMS, 1984—The only Miss America to be canned (for posing for sexually explicit photographs)

2. NORMA SMALLWOOD, 1926—Known as Mistress America for her private life

3. BETTE COOPER, 1937—Escaped from Atlantic City hours after she was crowned and refused to serve

4. HENRIETTA LEAVER, 1935—Exposed as having posed for a nude statue and not invited back to crown her successor

5. MARGARET GORMAN, 1921—Flattest Miss America, measuring 30–25–32

—Special to *The Worst of Everything* from Frank Deford, senior writer for *Sports Illustrated* and author of *There She Is: The Life and Times of Miss America*.

But what a strange muddle of daughter, sexpot, and platitude-tossing commentator we seek in our dream girls. I say dump the so-called talent and poise categories and give an honest rating of flesh. And, please, stop expecting them to be virgins.

Colorless Color Men

The Worst Jocks-Turned-Announcers, According to Jack Craig

1. JOE GREENE—Hired because of the success of his Coke commercial, he was so confused as a football analyst for CBS that he finally tried to script lines to fit every possible play. He lasted, barely, for a single season.

2. JOHNNY UNITAS—There was quite a contrast between letting his performance do the talking on the field and letting his tongue do the talking on the air. He survived for several years at NBC because, after all, he was Johnny U.

3. JOHNNY PESKY—Among the legion of baseball's good ol' boys handed a microphone, he may have been the most miscast. An entire generation of Red Sox fans grew up listening to his audible groans and cheers as a TV backdrop.

4. ALMOST ALL NHL ANALYSTS—Grammar, especially verb-noun relationship, was a low priority when these hulks spent all day on the ice as little tykes. Add cliches and half-sentences, and the audience must either laugh or turn down the audio.

—Special to *The Worst of Everything* from Jack Craig, TV sports columnist for the *Boston Globe*.

We're not talking play-by-play men here, or surely we'd honor Kiner, Rizzuto, and let's not forget Jerry Coleman in San Diego, who is quoted as having said, during a Padres game, "Winfield chases the ball. His head hits the wall. It's rollin' back toward the infield."

Bigger Not Better

Bill Caulkins's Worst-Shapes Hall of Fame

ANDY ROONEY.

THE ENTIRE FACTS OF LIFE CAST—The show should be renamed *The Fats of Life*.

RAYMOND BURR—He's the new Orson Welles.

WILLARD SCOTT—He has a high-pressure line forming at his belt line.

ROGER EBERT—He should spend more time "at the movies" than at the snack bar.

HOWARD COSELL.

SIMON LE BON.

TYNE DALEY—She's two-thirds of *Cagney and Lacey*.

WILLIAM (REFRIGERATOR) PERRY.

———————

—Selected by Bill Caulkins, fitness trainer to the stars.

This guy is downright nasty, a man after Andy Rooney's heart as well as his belt-line baggage.

Love a Man in Uniform, Hate Him out of It

The 5 Worst-Dressed Professional Athletes,
According to John Schulian

1. DAVE KINGMAN, FORMER OUTFIELDER, OAKLAND ATH-
   LETICS—Once the owner of slacks that barely reached the
   top of his socks, Dave is always a candidate to win the Rag-
   gedy Andy look-alike contest.

2. KIKI VANDEWEGHE, FORWARD, PORTLAND TRAIL BLAZERS
   —His wardrobe of sweatshirts and jeans had his former
   teammates in Denver threatening to pass the hat for him.

3. JOHN RIGGINS, FORMER FULLBACK, WASHINGTON REDSKINS
   —All the camouflage clothes in the world wouldn't hide
   his dubious taste.

4. HULK HOGAN, PROFESSIONAL WRESTLER—Who selects
   your formal wear, Hulk, the same person who does Cyndi
   Lauper's hair?

5. BILL BRADLEY, FORMER FORWARD, NEW YORK KNICKS,
   NOW DEMOCRATIC SENATOR, NEW JERSEY—To see him
   as a senior senator from New Jersey is to remember him
   as he was a decade ago with the New York Knicks—rum-
   pled, unbuttoned, and scuffed.

—From *GO*, January 1986.

*Mr. Schulian neglects to mention, wisely, the particular fac-
tors which have influenced these athletes in the evolution of their
dishabille, remarkable even among a group of singularly badly
educated and tasteless young men. (We're not talking the Senate
here—that's old men—but the locker room.) Kingman happens
to be widely acknowledged as the surliest bad-fielding strikeout
oaf of his day, though Riggins by passing out and insulting Sandra
Day O'Connor, all in one evening, comes in a close second. Hogan
is paid to act like a jerk. Vandeweghe plays no defense, so his
mode of dressing is yet another way for him to stress the offen-
sive. Bradley was never willing to spend a cent for anything, hence*

his nickname, "Dollar Bill." As an honest politician, he certainly has no money to spend on clothes now.

Hey, Imelda, Lend Me Your Pumps

The Worst in Fashion in 1987, According to Elizabeth Sporkin

UNWEARABLE MINISKIRTS—"Fashion designers couldn't stick with modest minis. For the spring collections shown in October, they went nuts with clothes that were obscenely short, tourniquet-tight, too bare, ridiculously frilly, and generally unwearable except to nightclubs or New Year's Eve parties."

TAMMY FAYE BAKKER—"Even a makeover didn't much help Tammy Faye, who slathered more makeup on her face than is sold in all of Woolworth's. Luckily, she didn't inspire any disciples to adopt her drag-queen look, though she did help bring back false eyelashes."

BALDNESS TREATMENTS—"Goos such as Nutriplexx by Aramis, Flowlin by Shiseido and Foltene by Minnetonka became the male equivalent of highly successful wrinkle creams."

WORKING WOMEN'S FASHIONS—"Too sexy styles and too many frills spelled professional suicide."

HOOD ORNAMENT JEWELRY—"Teens should have said no to this rock 'n roll fad."

"DENTAL FLOSS" SWIMSUITS—"Sorry but we just can't illustrate this style...."

—From *USA Today*, December 16, 1987.

Would You Buy a Used Car from Dick Nixon?

The 6 Great Casting Mistakes by Major Advertisers

1. Eleanor Roosevelt for Parkay Margarine

2. Buzz Aldrin for Volkswagen

3. Ronald Reagan for Van Heusen shirts

4. John Wayne for Datril

5. Mark Spitz for Gillette

6. Marilyn Chambers for Ivory Snow

—From Jeffrey Feinman, *The Money Lists*, Doubleday, Dolphin, New York, 1981.

I wouldn't have bought a Polaroid from Larry Olivier either, or a Renault from George C. Scott, even if Patton had ordered me to. But I would still love to see Nixon in a commercial. Is it too late? Ty-d-bol? Wite-Out? Say it ain't so, Dickie.

The Annoying Planet

The 5 Worst Animals to Film, According to David Attenborough

1. THREE-TOED SLOTH—It spends two-thirds of its entire life asleep, and even when it wakes up, it moves extremely slowly.

2. GRAHAM'S TILAPIA—This small fish lives in the scalding-hot volcanic springs in the middle of a lake of solid soda in Kenya.

3. DUCKBILLED PLATYPUS LAYING AN EGG—No one has ever seen it happen, but it is thought to take place in a burrow. The mother supposedly incubates it by curling herself around it.

4. EMPEROR PENGUIN INCUBATING AN EGG—It does it in one of the coolest places on earth, the Antarctic, in mid-winter when it is continuously dark for weeks on end.

5. DARWIN'S FROG BEING BORN—It hops out of its father's mouth after having hatched and lived as a tadpole in his

vocal sac; but unfortunately, the father gives no indication of when it is going to happen, and it is over in a fraction of a second.

—Special to *The Worst of Everything* from David Attenborough, zoologist, author, and creator-producer of *The Living Planet* and *Life on Earth* television series.

The man is not to be doubted. On the other hand, how many of these creatures ever had a drug problem, walked out on a contract, or tried to get a girlfriend or boyfriend a part? Tilapia don't even have a union. I checked.

Misery en Scene

The 5 Worst Directors of All Time, According to Tom Cunniff

1. EDWARD WOOD, JR.—His most famous movie, *Planet 9 from Outer Space* is the worst movie of all time, the *Citizen Kane* of bad movies.

2. PHIL TUCKER—The sad thing is he actually believed in the artistic integrity of his film *Robot Monster*.

3. ROGER CORMAN—Except for an adaptation of Poe's *The Pit and the Pendulum,* he filmed a lot of dumb and laughable movies. I'm sure he just stuck his name on *Tidal Wave*, where he dubbed Lorne Greene in Japanese-disaster footage, as ponderous as Alpo commercials.

4. WILLIAM "ONE-SHOT" BEAUDINE—The antithesis of Michael Cimino, who needed 40 takes for every scene, Beaudine shot everything just once, regardless of how obvious the mistakes were. He invented the western horror genre with *Jesse James Meets Frankenstein* and *Billy the Kid Meets the Werewolf.*

5. JENNOT SZWARC—A French director of American films, god knows why he was allowed to do *Santa Claus: The*

Movie, a $50-million fiasco, after such a notable loser as *Jaws 2.* He must have been as surprised as anyone by the *Santa Claus* gift.

———

—Special to *The Worst of Everything* from *People* film critic, Tom Cunneff.

Who Put the Boom in the....

The 4 Worst Technical Goofs in Films

1. *Carmen Jones*—The camera tracks Dorothy Dandridge down a street and the entire film crew is reflected in a shop window.

2. *The Wrong Box*—The roofs of Victorian London are emblazoned with television aerials.

3. *Decameron Nights*—Louis Jourdan stands on the deck of his fourteenth-century pirate ship, and a white truck rumbles down a hill in the background.

4. *Ancient Times*—The movie is set in the times of Boadicea, yet a wristwatch is clearly visible on one of the leading characters.

———

—From *Halliwell's Filmgoer's Companion* by Leslie Halliwell, Grenada Publishers Ltd., London, England, 1984.

Blockbusters for Blockheads

The 7 All-Time Dumb Movie Box-Office Champions, According to Variety Magazine

	Take, Millions
1. *Porky's*	$160
2. *Animal House*	$150
2. *Police Academy*	$150

4. *Stripes*	$ 85
5. *Meatballs*	$ 70
6. *Caddyshack*	$ 60
7. *Porky's II*	$ 55

—From *Variety*, June 10, 1985.

I'd add Beverly Hills Cop II and much of the Star Trek series, all the Friday the 13th series, and their ilk. In fact, once you get started, it's tough to stop naming bad popular movies. But going to them is another matter. Would that a few of our demented teens felt that way. Then maybe Hollywood would stop making them. Teenagers could get back to doing violence, vice, and vandalism instead of watching them.

On the Screen, off the Wall

*Michael Blowen's Nominees
for the Worst Films of 1987**

WORST PICTURE

Ernest Goes to Camp
Burglar
Ishtar
The Secret of My Success
Million Dollar Mystery

WORST ACTOR

Ernest V. Worrell—*Ernest Goes to Camp*
Tom Hanks—*Dragnet*
Bill Cosby—*Leonard, Part VI*
Bruce Willis—*Blind Date*
Michael J. Fox—*The Secret of My Success*

WORST ACTRESS

Melinda Dillon—*Harry and the Hendersons*
Helen Slater—*The Believers*

Whoopi Goldberg—*Burglar*
Helen Slater—*The Secret of My Success*
Valerie Kaprisky—*Meduses*

WORST SCREENPLAY

Dale Launer—*Blind Date*
Jim Cash, Jack Epps, Jr., and A. J. Carothers—*The Secret of My Success*
Elaine May—*Ishtar*
Tim Metcalfe, Miguel Tejada-Flores, and Rudy Deluca—*Million Dollar Mystery*
David Mamet—*The Untouchables*

WORST FOREIGN FILM

Straight from Hell—England
One Woman or Two—France
Man Facing Southeast—Argentina
Meduses—France
The Death of Mario Ricci—Italy

*Selections are as of July 1, 1987.

—Special to *The Worst of Everything* from Michael Blowen, film critic for the *Boston Globe*.

Mr. Blowen envisions an alternative Oscar ceremony to celebrate this crème de la sour crème. I'd watch the show. Problem is, as he acknowledges, most of these guys and gals take themselves far too seriously to show up, even for a chance to wink at the camera.

You Paid to See That?

The 10 Worst Movies of 1987, According to Mike Clark

The Allnighter—"It seemed far longer than that."
Beyond Therapy—"Robert Altman butchers Christopher Durang—and reconfirms that he has long since ceased making films for audiences."

Date with an Angel—"When she rings you up, claim you have a splitting headache."

Fatal Beauty—"Whoopi Goldberg blasts us point blank with sass and bullets: is this the way to become a beloved screen comedienne?"

Gardens of Stone—"The complete, hopefully temporary, collapse of Francis Coppola makes this the year's most depressing movie."

The Hanoi Hilton—"Film Making Fundamentals 101—the way to portray tedium is *not* to make the only '87 film more tedious than Michael Cimino's *The Sicilian*."

Harry and the Hendersons—"I hear even the ASPCA is recommending this bigfoot be put to slow death."

Jaws—The Revenge—"In a year of *Superman IV*, *Police Academy IV*, and *Death Wish IV*— the year's worst sequel."

Over the Top—"With this megastinker, Sly Stallone's 'body of work' now becomes punier than Anthony Michael Hall."

Straight to Hell and *Walker*—"Why waste valuable space by making them individual slots? Alex Cox (Sid and Nancy) did both."

—From *USA Today*, December 18, 1987.

Bye Bye Broadway

The Worst in Theater for 1987, According to Jack Curry

Worst play—"The grim retirement home comedy/drama *A Month of Sundays*, starring Jason Robards, lasted nowhere near as long as the title would suggest."

Worst musical hit—"Hyped to the skies, the Andrew Lloyd Webber–Trevor Nunn musical *Starlight Express* turned out to be a boom box of a show. It's shiny, high tech, loud and empty."

Worst single performance—"Georgia Brown, in Roza's title

role, should know better than to sing like a buzzsaw and look like a drag queen."

Most luxurious trip to nowhere—"*Tamara*: the ride is great, but what's the point?"

—From *USA Today*, December 18, 1987.

Curtains for You

The Fastest-Closing Broadway Shows of 1987

		Dates
1.	*A Month of Sundays*	April 16–18
2.	*Broadway*	June 25–27
3.	*Late Night Comic*	October 15–17
4.	*Sleight of Hand*	May 3–9
5.	*Harvey Fierstein's Safe Sex*	April 5–12
6.	*Roza*	October 1–11

—From the League of American Theaters and Producers.

Producers are always complaining that bad opening-night reviews kill their shows before the audiences have a chance to see for themselves. Why doesn't anyone thank the critics for saving us from these disasters, if that's the case? And why don't producers show the script to a few critics and regular folk before they invest sacdillions in theatrical turkeys? Beats me. Thank god the British keep the American musical theater going.

Something Else Must Be On

The 10 Least-Watched TV Shows of 1987

		Rating*
1.	*Once a Hero*	4.6
2.	*Leg Work*	6.2
3.	*Everything's Relative*	6.5
4.	*Max Headroom*	6.9
5.	*West 57th*	7.0
6.	*My Sister Sam*	7.3
7.	*Sledge Hammer!*	7.6
7.	*Sable*	7.6
9.	*The Charmings*	8.1
10.	*CBS Saturday Night Movie*	8.3

*One rating point equals 886,000 TV households.

—A. C. Nielsen Co. ratings.

I wish I could say I missed all these; however, I did see a few and even liked every episode of #4 I caught. As a vegetarian I passed on #7—I didn't think a history of fur trading would be all that engrossing.

Don't Look Now

The Worst in TV for 1987, According to Monica Collins

WORST RETURNING DRAMA—*Moonlighting* "Now the ABC series that once defied description has settled into another category all its own—boring."

WORST DRAMA FOR ANY BABY BOOMER WHO HAS AN AMERICAN EXPRESS GOLD CARD AND COUCH-POTATO CACHET —NBC's *Hunter*. Would you admit to sitting home Saturday nights and watching it?

WORST DRESSER IN A DRAMA —"Mary Beth Lacey in CBS's *Cagney and Lacey*. The policewoman played by Tyne Daley might as well wear burlap bags and cardboard jewelry."

WORST LEAVE-HER-FOR-DEAD EPISODE IN A DRAMA—"The *Colbys* cliffhanger last spring in which Fallon met a UFO. The *Dynasty* spinoff never came back to ABC after that gruesome, embarrassingly bad episode."

WORST ROMANTIC DRAMA LEAD—"James Brolin of ABC's *Hotel*. Better to order from room service."

WORST OLD-SHOE COMEDY—"CBS gave *The Morning Program* the boot after less than a year. It was excessively cozy and cheery, as if convinced that Mariette Hartley could go on chirping fatuously forever."

WORST NBC THURSDAY NIGHT COMEDY—"*A Different World*. Lisa Bonet plays a college kid who sleepwalks her way through academia's ups and downs."

WORST NEW COMEDY—"*Everything's Relative*. Can we quote ourselves here: 'A barking turkey.' Well, before Thanksgiving, the turkey had barked itself into cancellation oblivion."

TV JOURNALIST YOU'RE EMBARRASSED TO SPEND TIME WITH —"Who else? The intrepid Geraldo Rivera. . . . Rivera, along with some stage-struck cops, staged his own drug raid, live and on-camera. The result? A lawsuit."

WORST TV SERIES FOR EXAMINING YOUR NAVEL BY —"ABC's *thirtysomething*. Just a lot of yuppies running around taking everything too seriously."

—From *USA Today*, December 15, 1987

I like Monica Collins better than anything on TV, including the other Ms. Collins. But I do like thirtysomething, as her description fits both me and the show pretty well.

We'll Be Right Back with Charo

The 5 Worst Talk-Show Hosts of All Time

We've grown up, grown old, at least grown sleepy watching them or using them as nightlights to reproduce by. Hosting is an impossible job, complicated by a parade of commercials and has-been entertainer-guests who show up for union minimum. Yet some have gone beyond the mere call of duty to create true narcolepsy-inducing drugs of frightening ennui. My own selections:

1. REGIS PHILBIN—That this man is any closer to the entertainment industry than an aluminum-siding salesperson is remarkable in itself, but hosting a national show? Anyone who has had to laugh at Joey Bishop deserves pity, but not a microphone.

2. OPRAH WINFREY—If you want loud, fat, and crude, go to a wrestling match. The woman lies about her dress size (she's a 14 like the Queen Mary is a dinghy), makes fun of the diction of some of her own minority, and invites all manner of deviants and murdering scum onto her show so she can express outrage at their behavior, then cuts to commercials. And she loves Barbara Walters. For this we make her rich?

3. JOAN RIVERS—She looks like a ghost, talks like a sailor, and has all the on-air empathy of a young Klaus Barbie. This qualified her in the minds of Fox Broadcasting's foxy executives to be the cornerstone of their new network. These same savants are now paying her millions not to go on. That is one cause to which we would contribute.

4. JOEY BISHOP—Watching him is like watching your father play cards and kibitz, in slow motion. The man was ahead of his time as an entertainer: At 50 he acted like he was 80. Small wonder he needed a sidekick to provide appreciative laughs, and that no one more talented than Regis Philbin (see above) could be found to take the job.

5. JACK PAAR—A man of boundless ego and talent so bounded it could fit in Pee-Wee Herman's shorts. A jittery sycophant whose greatest claim to fame is standing by while Judy Garland made a drunken fool of herself. He had good reason to be nervous, and to quit the business before his patient audience sent him packing.

Pulling the Plug

The 30 Worst TV Shows of All Time

1. *The Baileys of Balboa*—"This had to be seen not to be believed," wrote John Horn, *New York Herald Tribune.*

2. *Beacon Hill*—"Commercial television once again refusing to trust the intelligence of its audience," wrote Richard Schickel, *Time.*

3. *The Big Party*—"*The Big Party* is a big bore," wrote Dwight Whitney of *TV Guide.*

4. *The Dakotas*—"There are so many good guys that, between you, me, and the hitching post, we didn't even trust the commercials," wrote Cleveland Amory, *TV Guide.*

5. *Get Christie Love*—"Drenched with inadequate scripts, listless direction, and a preposterous concept," wrote *Daily Variety.*

6. *Gilligan's Island*—"It's hard to know where to begin to criticize the program. It's best to begin by switching channels," wrote Frank Judge of the *Detroit News.*

7. *Hee Haw*—"It's so bad, it's an insult to the intelligence of a nursery school dropout," wrote Eleanor Roberts of the *Boston Herald Traveler.*

8. *Hogan's Heroes*—"I consider it distinctly sick," wrote Henry Mitchell, *Memphis Commercial-Appeal.*

9. *Jackpot Bowling*—"A monumental bore," wrote Melvin Durslag, *TV Guide*.

10. *The Jerry Lewis Show*—"Patent gracelessness...a telethon of vapidity. The star needs instruction in remedial conversation," wrote Jack Gould, *New York Times*.

11. *Land of the Giants*—"Looks like it was written in thirty minutes over a pastrami sandwich," wrote Rex Reed.

12. *The Liberace Show*—"The biggest sentimental vomit of all time," wrote William Connor, *London Daily Mirror*.

13. *Me and the Chimp*—"Represents a new depth in TV programming," said Fred Silverman, programming executive.

14. *Mickey*—"The lowest grade of tired slapstick, wornout comedy gimmicks, exhausted dialogue," wrote Terry Turner, *Chicago Daily News*.

15. *Miss America Pageants*—"Dull and pretentious and racist and exploitative and icky and sad," wrote Shana Alexander in *Life*.

16. *My Living Doll*—"One long, tiresome, leering joke," wrote Anthony LaCamera, *Boston Herald American*.

17. *My Mother, the Car*—"The premiere made a strong case for not fastening your seatbelts," wrote Jack Gould, *New York Times*.

18. *The Newlywed Game*—"Tripe...an insult to the sensibilities and a low-water mark on TV's achievement pole," wrote Lee Margulies, *Los Angeles Times*.

19. *O.K. Crackerby*—"Nothing has appalled me as much as the premise...that money can buy everything," wrote Harry Harris, *Philadelphia Inquirer*.

20. *The Pruitts of Southampton*—"It would be nothing less than a Chinese torture to have to put up with this woefully uninspired nonsense week after week...." wrote Win Fanning, *Pittsburgh Post-Gazette*.

21. *Queen for a Day*—"...a chamber of horrors," said *TV Guide*.

22. *The Sammy Davis, Jr., Show*—"Television has rarely seen such a bust," said *Time*.

23. *Satins and Spurs*—"...a lot of perspiration, but no inspiration," said *The Hollywood Reporter*.

24. *Supermarket Sweep*—"Daytime paean to human greed," said *Variety*.

25. *The Survivors*—"There is not a character, a situation, a line of dialogue that is remotely associated with human beings," write Cecil Smith, *Los Angeles Times*.

26. *S.W.A.T.*—"Should stand for Simplistic, Warlike, and Totalitarian," said *People*.

27. *The Tammy Grimes Show*—"Plotting for morons by morons," wrote Harry Harris, *Philadelphia Inquirer*.

28. *Three's Company*—"Inane, cheap sexual humor which is about as subtle as a mugging, and about as funny," wrote Lee Margulies, *Los Angeles Times*.

29. *Turn On*—"Looks like a half-hour reject from the Rowan and Martin memory bank," said *Time*.

30. *You're in the Picture*—"The biggest disaster since the Johnstown Flood," said *TV Guide*.

—From Bart Andrews and Brad Dunning, *The Worst TV Shows Ever*, Dutton, New York, 1980.

Ground Ol' Opry

The Worst in Country Music for 1987, According to David Zimmerman

JOHNNY CASH—*Johnny Cash Is Coming to Town*—"Oddball song choices like "Heavy Metal" make this disappointing album by a revered performer as corny as its title."

OAK RIDGE BOYS—*Where the Fast Lane Ends*—"This was made while William Lee Golden was being forced out of the group. Not a good time to harmonize."

BARBARA MANDRELL—*Sure Feels Good*—"Forced emotionalism and mawkish songs."

MERLE HAGGARD AND WILLIE NELSON—*Seashores of Old Mexico*—"Two old pals get together and produce an album and forget to follow through."

KRIS KRISTOFFERSON—*Repossessed*—"Methinks this album protests too much for all but the most politicized stereo systems."

—From *USA Today*, December 18, 1987.

Another Country for This Country Music

The 10 Worst Country Music Songs, According to Alanna Nash

1. "Coward of the County," Kenny Rogers—An insultingly trite, formulaic story-song written by someone whose idea of country people comes from watching *The Beverly Hillbillies*. Delivered by the most hackneyed singer in the history of country music.

2. "Me and Little Andy," Dolly Parton—The story of a girl and her dog who go to the big kennel in the sky. One of the most cloyingly sentimental songs ever conjured, and proof that even Dolly Parton needs corrective surgery once in a while.

3. "Teddy Bear," Red Sovine—This 4-hanky tale of a crip-

pled kid, his CB radio, and a friendly trucker is enough to turn anybody into an axe-murderer. Sovine had a fatal attack after this record came out. See, it even got to him.

4. "As Soon As I Hang Up the Phone," Conway Twitty and Loretta Lynn—Loretta Lynn may be a national treasure but you'd have to have Crisco in your brain not to think this is dreck.

5. "War Is Hell on the Homefront, Too," T. G. Sheppard —Hot-flash fantasy for the crotchless-panty set.

6. "God Bless the USA," Lee Greenwood—Jive, slick-patina patriotism from a former Las Vegas casino dealer who can't even grow a decent beard.

7. "The Rubber Room," Porter Wagoner—The Wagon-master's idea of what it would be like in solitary confinement at the Funny Farm. From the sound of it, Porter's spent some time there already. Or needs to.

8. "Me and the Animals," Bobby Goldsboro—The touching story of a spurned lover who dumps all his problems on the honkers at the zoo. Goldsboro, of "Honey" fame, was accused of abusing his own daughter a few years ago in a messy divorce case. Apparently, zebras weren't enough for him.

9. "Peel Me a Nanner," Roy Drusky—Sure, Kong, anything you say.

10. "Tomb of the Unknown Love," Kenny Rogers—C'mon, tomb of the unknown love? Winner of my personal Conehead Award for Dumbest Record of All Time.

—Special to *The Worst of Everything* from Alanna Nash, country music critic for *Stereo Review* and author of *Dolly*, a biography of country queen Dolly Parton, and *Talking with the Legends of Country Music*.

Country music aficionados seem to take offense at everything, so Ms. Nash's well-considered list will probably upset them. I think she went very easy on a genre that has attained new lows in an industry full of nadirs in song titles ("I Got the Hungries for Your Love and I'm Waiting on Your Welfare Line" was my favorite) lyrics, tawdry getups, and twanging accompaniments, highs in bouffants, syrupy sentiment, false piousness, and teary addiction confessions.

It Should Have Ended before the Fat Lady Sang

The 5 Most Overrated Classical Music Compositions, According to Herbert Kupferberg

1. Puccini's *Tosca*—This is the only bad opera he wrote.

2. Richard Strauss's *Elektra*—This is one of the several bad operas he wrote.

3. Brahms's *Requiem*—George Bernard Shaw said it was borne patiently only by the corpse.

4. Liszt's *Two Piano Concertos*—They're of interest mainly to pianists.

5. All of Bruckner's Symphonies.

—Special to *The Worst of Everything* from Herbert Kupferberg, senior editor of *Parade* and author of *The Book of Classical Music Lists*.

Were he considering underrated compositions, I trust Mr. Kupferberg would include PDQ Bach's Concerto in C Minus and Iphigenia in Brooklyn, two of my favorite classical works. If we had more people writing such as this for the French and bicycle horns maybe we wouldn't need "Rock Me Amadeus."

When the 'Aints Go Marchin' In

The Worst in Rock Videos for 1987, According to Edna Gunderson

MICHAEL JACKSON—*Bad* and *The Way You Make Me Feel*. "The former stereotypes black youths as hoodlums; the latter exalts macho street posturing."

FAT BOYS AND THE BEACH BOYS—*Wipeout*. "Rotund rappers in Hawaiian shirts do not belong on TV. Even wide-screen TV."

HEART—*Alone*. "Literally the year's most overexposed video. Gratuitous lingering shots of Nancy Wilson's cleavage, dramatic close ups of Ann Wilson's face in a continuing attempt to hide her fat."

BILLY IDOL—*Mony Mony*. "The guy needs his bratty sneer surgically reduced."

DEBBIE GIBSON—*Shake Your Love*. "Oooh, how novel. A sock hop! Makes soft drink commercials seem artistic."

———

—From *USA Today*, December 18, 1987.

Music to Snore By

The 10 Most Boring Musical Compositions

1. Vivaldi: *The Four Seasons*

2. Ravel: *Bolero*

3. Pachelbel: Kanon in D

4. Orff: *Carmina Burana*

5. Glass: Various works

6. Tchaikovsky: Symphony No. 5 in E Minor

7. Dvorak: Symphony No. 9 in E Minor, *New World*

8. Liszt: *Les Preludes*

9. Bruckner: Symphony No. 9 in D Minor

10. Ives: *Three Places in New England*

—Selected in a 1984 poll of readers of *Keynote*.

Throw in a sonorous 3-hour introduction by Robert J. Lurtsema (take my word for it if you don't pick up his vibes on your box) and you've got yourself one great nap.

It's Curtains for Us Now

The 6 Most Disastrous Musical Performances

1. Gretry, *Richard, Coeur de Lion*—The aria "O Richard! O mon roi!" played a part in precipitating the French Revolution. When news of Marie Antoinette's singing of the aria at a banquet in Versailles reached Paris, indignant mobs marched to Versailles to demand the royal family return to Paris.

2. Rossini, *The Barber of Seville*—At the opera's premiere at Teatro Argentina in Rome, February 20, 1816, a string on Almaviva's guitar snapped during an aria, Basilio tripped over a trapdoor, and a cat wandered onstage during the finale. The audience hooted and hissed, and Rossini fled the theater, fearing assassination.

3. Auber, *Masaniello, or La Muette de Portici*—When first performed in 1828 in Brussels, then occupied by the Dutch, the opera's scenes of patriotic fervor ignited a popular uprising that led to Belgian independence.

4. Verdi, *A Masked Ball*—Censorship issues over the depiction of the assassination of a royal personage in this 1859 opera stirred up patriotic feelings among Italians, who shouted Verdi's name in the streets and scrawled it on walls.

5. Stravinsky, *The Rite of Spring*—Premiered May 29, 1913, at Theatre des Champs Elysees in Paris, the work was

poorly received, catcalls and stamping of feet greeted early measures, then fistfights and shoving matches broke out.

6. Fritz Kreisler's Cornell Concert—The arrival of the ex-Austrian Army violinist in December 1919 was greeted with denunciations by Ithaca's mayor. The concert was held despite the fact that electrical wires were cut and fistfights broke out in the audience.

—From *The Book of Classical Music Lists* by Herbert Kupferberg.

Performing Live?

The 3 Worst Concert Performers, According to Steve Morse

MOTLEY CRUE—A mindless metal band teeming with cliches, sexist stage jokes, and bland musicianship.

ABBA—Some of their records have been monuments to poor craftwork, but in concert the group was unmasked as trite and treacly.

CHUCK BERRY—The Hall of Famer has made some great records, but never travels with a band. Hence, some nights can be sloppy nightmares.

The 5 Worst Groups, According to Steve Morse

POWER STATION
ANGEL
ASIA
RAINBOW
STARSHIP (latter-day version)

—Special to *The Worst of Everything* from Steve Morse, music critic for the *Boston Globe*.

If you disagree, take it up with Mr. Morse, not me. The last concert I went to was Sly and the Family Stone, ca. 1971. Mr. Stone showed up looking as if he wanted to live up to his name, 3 hours late and unable to remember the lyrics to songs he had written, which were hardly of Jacques Brel complexity. I would have demanded my money back if I hadn't gate-crashed to get in.

Weasel Goes the Pop

The Worst in Pop Music for 1987, According to Edna Gunderson

BRUCE WILLIS—*The Return of Bruno*. "At least the minimally gifted Blues Brothers treated soul music with reverence. Willis is shamelessly self-absorbed. And he can't sing. Period."

DAVID BOWIE—*Never Let Me Down*. "The chameleon, struggling again to confound expectations, loves himself in a self-conscious Tom Jones disguise."

NEIL DIAMOND—*Hot August Night II*. "A tepid sequel to 1972's LP. Too much of a bad thing."

LITTLE STEVEN—*Freedom No Compromise*. "Former E Streeter screams murky political rhetoric at a feverish (and unharmonious) pitch."

SUZANNE VEGA—*Solitude Standing*. "Folk singer *ordinaire*, with the grating whimper of an injured Lassie. Literary conceit more suited to college anthologies than pop charts."

—From *USA Today*, December 18, 1987.

If You Like Judith Krantz...

The 5 Most Overrated Contemporary Authors, According to Peter Prescott

1. KURT VONNEGUT, JR., AND HIS SUCCESSOR, KURT VONNEGUT—There was a time, shortly before anyone had read *Slaughterhouse-Five*, when it looked as if Vonnegut might turn some kind of corner and become a writer adults would

want to read. Instead, he chose to pander to the teenagers who had made a cult figure of him. He never recovered.

2. JOHN GARDNER—Another writer much fancied by the Pepsi generation. He did write one fine novel, *Grendel*, which did well enough to allow him to release his juvenilia (*Sunlight Dialogues*), some stilted fiction, and finally some books which contained plagiarized passages.

3. BARBARA TUCHMAN—Another writer who wrote one book (*The Guns of August*) so good that readers tended not to look closely at what came after: her ill-proportioned biography of Stilwell and her often wrongheaded introduction to fourteenth-century history and thought.

4. GORE VIDAL—I count 2 good novels among his many: *Myra Breckinridge* and *Burr*. But it's the praise his essays have received that interests me most: The essays are, in fact, exceedingly smooth, but for all Vidal's attitudinizing, they lack any kind of moral, intellectual, or aesthetic center. Vidal's witty writing conveys an essentially trivial mind. The effect would be pleasing if he didn't imply that his sensitivity is superior to everyone else's.

5. DORIS LESSING—How long has it been since she wrote a good book? Was *The Golden Notebook* the last one? And how many books has she foisted off on us since then? I've lost count.

—Special to *The Worst of Everything* from Peter Prescott, *Newsweek* senior book critic.

I don't think Mr. Prescott is going to get much argument, except from the above, since the average American reads no books a year. I know I only read these authors when I had to for school, and they were too contemporary to come with Monarch notes. I trust the crib sheets have caught up by now. If not, perhaps the contemporary literature teachers have wised up.

Better Dead Than Read

The Worst Books for 1987, According to Robert Wilson

FICTION

All We Need of Hell by Harry Crews—"After I called this 'a repellent little book' in a review, Crews told *People* magazine that he wanted to 'tear off my head and puke in my lungs,' which gives you a good sense of the level of taste of the book itself."

Answered Prayers by Truman Capote—"A fragment of a novel that should never have been written, much less published."

A Cannibal in Manhattan by Tama Janowitz—"Let's pretend that Tama Janowitz, Brett Easton Ellis and Jill Eisenstadt never happened, shall we?"

Serenissima: A Novel of Venice by Erica Jong—"*Fear of Flying* has its pound of flesh from *Merchant of Venice*."

Hot Flashes by Barbara Raskin—"Even the title causes a blush."

Alnilum by James Dickey—"The bloated meets the blind."

NONFICTION

Miami by Joan Didion—"At least her *Salvador* suggests she actually went there; this reads like notes from the *Miami Herald*."

Women and Love: A Cultural Revolution in Progress by Shere Hite—"Muddled thinking and mangled writing. You'll get more insight from Oprah on an off day."

—From *USA Today*, December 19, 1987.

See Spot Die

The 6 Worst Children's Books, According
to **Parents' Choice**

1. *Show Me* by Will McBride and Helga Fleischhauer-Hardt —"Art" photos of nude children and adults, and writing that is hard-core psycho-babble...an intellectual's approach to child abuse.

2. *Little Black Sambo* by Helen Bannerman—For all the pain it has caused.

3. *The Dick and Jane Series* by Abby Robinson—See Dick dislike reading. See Jane's self-esteem shrivel. Run, kids, run.

4. Beatrix Potter Stories with Any Illustrator Other Than Ms. Potter—These are almost perfect stories and should never be changed.

5. *Myth That Masquerades as Science* and Other Gabler Texts

6. Books Published as Children's Books Because Nobody Can Figure a Way to Otherwise Market Them

------

—Special to *The Worst of Everything* from Diana Huss Green, editor-in-chief of *Parents' Choice.*

However bad today's kiddie-lit list looks, this is one realm where your parents truly had it worse. When I reached the age of consent, my mother showed me the copy of Struwwelpeter that had been read to her as a Teutonic tot. This classic featured every means of torture known to Papa Doc or the Three Stooges. Sweet dreams, little Adolf.

Damn the Typesetter

The Worst Printed Book

Missae ac Missalis Anatomia—Published in 1561, this 172-page book contained 15 pages of errata. The author declared that the devil had made the printer do it.

—From M. Hirsh Goldberg, *The Blunder Book*, Morrow, New York, 1984.

Sistine Chapel by the Numbers

The 6 Most Overrated Artists, According to Paul Taylor

Cimabue
Michelangelo
Leonardo
Raphael
Pablo Picasso
Andy Warhol

Catholic artists all, they failed to achieve immortality in every sense but the artistic.

—Special to *The Worst of Everything* from New York–based art critic Paul Taylor.

You got me. Perhaps contemporary critics are catching up to contemporary arts when it comes to inscrutability. Maybe these guys were all Catholic; certainly they are all dead.

SPORTS
WORSTS

You were there when Franco Harris made his immaculate reception, when Bannister ran a sub-4-minute mile, when Williams hit Sewall's "ephus" pitch out of the park. You've seen, or have claimed to see, all of sport's finer moments. That is part of any fan's vicarious thrill of victory.

But where were you in the agony of defeat? When Lennie Merullo made 4 errors in 1 inning? When Darryl Dawkins broke a glass backboard before picking up his sixth foul? When Ilie Nastase mooned the referee? And if you were there, would you have cursed Bill Buckner, called Fred Merkle "bonehead," or sung the *Looney Tunes* theme for Jimmy Piersall?

No, not you. Here, then, is a side of sports you, in your gentlemanly or ladylike manner, have overlooked or forgotten: the dumbest baseball injuries, the most lopsided football games, the least distinguished boxing champions, the worst Hall of Famers.

In short, we give you the experts' view—if not Red Barber in the catbird's seat, then green vitriol from some cattier experts in nearly every sport and in some, like bowling, that aren't. Mayhaps their recollections will give you cause to remember that you were there for some of these epic moments, behaving as boorishly as thousands of others. If so, maybe Lennie Merullo won't be the only one with nightmares of E-6 flashing on the scoreboard as yet another grounder scoots through his legs.

WORSTS IN PROFESSIONAL BASEBALL

Let's Play One

The 5 Worst Days a Ballplayer Has Ever Suffered, According to Dan Okrent

1. SEPTEMBER 13, 1942—Chicago Cubs shortstop Lennie Merullo commits 4 errors in 1 inning.

2. MAY 1, 1920—In the longest game ever played, second baseman Charlie Pick of the Boston Braves goes hitless in 11 at-bats.

3. JULY 31, 1963—Pitcher Paul Foytack of the California Angels surrenders 4 consecutive home runs.

4. JULY 21, 1975—Joe Torre of the New York Mets comes to bat 4 times in a game, and each time grounds into a double play.

5. AUGUST 28, 1909—In the second inning of the first game of a doubleheader, pitcher Dolly Gray of the Washington Senators walks 8 batters, 7 of them consecutively. Three years later, Gray retires with a lifetime record of 17 wins and 52 defeats.

———

—Special to *The Worst of Everything* from Daniel Okrent, author of *The Ultimate Book of Baseball* and *Nine Innings* and editor of *New England Monthly*.

My sympathies to all these guys. Things could be worse. You could have been a 1960s Met or a 1980s Pirate. You could have the locker next to Darryl Strawberry or Jim Rice. You could have had Don Zimmer's affinity for the wall (or his haircut). You could have had the same travel agent as Pumpsie Green, or have had to back up Dick Stuart at first or bat against Ryne Duren. Or you could be the sportswriter who had to interview Steve Carlton or Dave Kingman.

Babe and Who Else?

The 10 Worst Trades in Baseball History, According to Brendan Boyd

1. The Boston Red Sox sold Babe Ruth to the New York Yankees for $125,000 and a $300,000 loan on January 3, 1920.

2. The Cincinnati Reds traded Christy Mathewson to the New York Giants for Amos Rusie on December 15, 1900.

3. The Chicago Cubs traded Lou Brock, Paul Toth, and Jack Spring to the St. Louis Cardinals for Ernie Broglio, Bobby Shantz, and Doug Clemens on June 15, 1964.

4. The Detroit Tigers traded Billy Pierce and $10,000 to the Chicago White Sox for Aaron Robinson on November 10, 1948.

5. The Cincinnati Reds traded Frank Robinson to the Baltimore Orioles for Milt Pappas, Jack Baldschun, and Dick Simpson on December 9, 1965.

6. The San Francisco Giants traded George Foster to the Cincinnati Reds for Frank Duffy and Vern Geishert on May 29, 1971.

7. The Philadelpia Phillies traded Grover Alexander and Bill Killefer to the Chicago Cubs for Mike Prendergast, Pickles Dillhoefer, and $55,000 on December 11, 1917.

8. The Montreal Expos traded Ken Singleton and Mike Torrez to the Baltimore Orioles for Dave McNally, Rich Coggins, and Bill Kirkpatrick on December 4, 1974.

9. The New York Giants traded Edd Roush, Christy Mathewson, and Bill McKechnie to the Cincinnati Reds for Buck Herzog and Red Killefer on July 20, 1916.

10. The St. Louis Cardinals traded Steve Carlton to the Philadelphia Phillies for Rick Wise on February 25, 1972.

—Special to *The Worst of Everything* from Brendan Boyd, co-author of *The Great American Baseball Card Trading Book.*

The Vestibule of Fame

The 10 Worst Baseball Hall of Famers, According to Brendan Boyd

1. Ralph Kiner

2. Hoyt Wilhelm

3. Chuck Klein

4. Johnny Mize

5. Don Drysdale

6. Harmon Killebrew

7. Monte Irvin

8. Duke Snider

9. Billy Herman

10. Hank Greenberg

—Special to *The Worst of Everything* from Brendan Boyd, co-author of *The Great American Baseball Card Trading Book*.

What do you suppose Mr. Boyd has done with his Topps cards of the above. Tossed a coin and lost them to some Gus Triandos leaners, I'll wager. And I doubt you'll catch him listening to Kiner's Korner either. I had forgotten Wilhelm was a Hall of Famer. I wasn't even sure, for that matter, he'd retired yet. If pitching qualified for assault with a deadly weapon, Drysdale would be in the Sing Sing Hall of Fame. His idea of pitching inside was behind the batter's head.

Say It Ain't "Horse Belly," Joe

The 10 Worst Nicknames in Baseball History, According to Brendan Boyd

1. Aloysius "Desperate" Beatty, New York Giants

2. Frank "Turkeyfoot" Brower, Washington Senators

3. George "Peasoup" Dumont, Washington Senators

4. Fred "Bootnose" Hofmann, New York Yankees

5. Charlie "Swamp Baby" Wilson, St. Louis Cardinals

6. Eric "Boob" McNair, Philadelphia Athletics

7. Wilbur "Raw Meat" Rodgers, Cincinnati Reds

8. Joseph "Horse Belly" Sargent, Detroit Tigers

9. Charles Busted "Lady" Baldwin, Brooklyn Dodgers

10. Wellington "Wingy" Quinn, Chicago Cubs

—Special to *The Worst of Everything* from Brendan Boyd, co-author of *The Great American Baseball Card Trading Book.*

And what about "Death to Flying Things"? Now there was a nickname.

One Pitch, Many Errors

The Worst Fielding Play in History

Mike Grady, third baseman, New York Giants, 1899, 4 errors on 1 ball:

ERROR 1—Grady bobbled a grounder, enabling the runner to reach first.
ERROR 2—Grady threw wild to first, and the runner advanced to second.
ERROR 3—The runner tried to stretch for third on Grady's overthrow. The first baseman threw to Grady, who covered the bag but dropped the ball.
ERROR 4—The runner rounded for home when Grady dropped the throw. Grady recovered the ball but overthrew the catcher. Run scored.

—From M. Hirsh Goldberg, *The Blunder Book*, Morrow, New York, 1984.

I like Grady's style. His instructions, no doubt, were to keep this hitter off the bases, and he did all he could to oblige.

It Ain't Over til It's Over

The Worst Yogi-isms, According to Yogi Himself

Berra claims never to have said the following things, widely attributed to him:

1. "If you can't imitate him, don't copy him." ("Stengel said that," says Yogi, "not me.")

2. When asked if he'd buy his kids an encyclopedia: "No, let them walk to school like I did."

3. When asked, "Are you a fatalist?": "No, I never collected postage stamps."

4. When asked about Mickey Mantle's switch hitting: "Mantle was naturally amphibious."

5. When told by a mayor's wife, "You look cool": "You don't look so hot yourself, ma'am."

6. When asked if he had seen *Dr. Zhivago:* "No, I feel fine."

Berra insists, however, that he did utter the following immortal words: "It ain't over till it's over." And "How can you think and hit at the same time?" On noting that teammate Bobby Brown was reading a medical textbook, "How does it turn out?" And "Nobody goes there anymore, it's too crowded" (although that line appeared first in a Dorothy Parker story).

—Special to *The Worst of Everything* from Yogi, ex-manager of the New York Yankees and a noted orator.

The question remains, is Yogi Berra the best authority on Yogi Berra? Perhaps we are confusing him with a figment of Joe Garagiola's imagination.

Two Strikes, You're Out (Part I)

The Worst Baseball Parks to Hit In, According to George Brett

1. CLEVELAND STADIUM—The batter's box is uncomfortable, the field isn't kept up, and it's windy.

2. OAKLAND-ALAMEDA STADIUM—It's damp and the ball doesn't carry well.

The best parks are in Kansas City and Anaheim.

—Special to *The Worst of Everything* from George Brett, third baseman for the Kansas City Royals and former American League batting champion.

Two Strikes, You're Out (Part II)

The Worst Baseball Parks to Hit In, According to Dave Winfield

1. HOUSTON ASTRODOME—The ball is dead there; it doesn't carry.

2. YANKEE STADIUM—The place is a graveyard, absolute death to right-handed power hitters.

The best parks are in Boston and Anaheim.

—Special to *The Worst of Everything* from Dave Winfield, outfielder for the New York Yankees.

Yankee, Go Homer

The 10 Worst Foreign Players in Japanese Baseball History

Position	Name	Year	Games Played	Ave	HR	RBI
P	Val Snow*	1974	DNP			
C	Nick Testa	1962	57	.136	0	5
1B	Joe Pepitone	1973	14	.163	1	2
2B	Frank Coggins	1973	13	.125	2	4
3B	Reno Bertola	1964	20	.175	1	2
SS	Chico Fernandez	1965	52	.144	1	8
OF	Buddy Bradford	1977	56	.192	4	11
OF	Paul Dade	1981	37	.219	1	5
OF	Frank Howard	1974	1	.000	0	0
DH	Charlie Spikes	1981	26	.122	1	2

*Val Snow, an ex-minor leaguer, paid his own way to Japan and landed a job with the Nippon Ham Fighters. He took his first salary check in advance and returned to Salt Lake City without pitching a game.

—Selected by the *Japanese Baseball Newsletter*.

As for Bob Horner, his 1-year results indicate that he was one import worth his considerable weight in gold—or in Kirin beer, in which he may have invested much of his gold.

Iron Glove

The Most Errors, by Position, in a Season

Position	Player	Errors
1B	Jack Doyle, New York Giants, 1900	43
2B	George Grantham, Chicago Cubs, 1923	150
3B	"Piano Legs" Hickman, New York Giants, 1900	91
SS	Rudy Hulswitt, Philadelphia Phillies, 1903	138
OF	Cy Seymour, Cincinnati Reds, 1903	36
C	Oscar Stanage, Detroit Tigers, 1911	41
P	Doc Newton, Cincinnati Reds, 1900	17

—From Joseph L. Reichler, *The Great All-Time Baseball Record Book*, Macmillan, New York, 1981.

We'll Get 'em Next Year

The Most Team Losses in a Season

	Games Lost
1. New York Mets, 1962	120
2. Philadelphia Athletics, 1916	117
3. Boston Braves, 1935	115
4. Washington Senators, 1904	113
5. Pittsburgh Pirates, 1952	112
6. Boston Red Sox, 1932	111
6. St. Louis Browns, 1939	111
6. Philadelphia Phillies, 1941	111
6. New York Mets, 1963	111

—From Joseph L. Reichler, *The Great All-Time Baseball Record Book*, Macmillan, New York, 1981.

There is something to be said for expansion, after all. No team has ever been as good as the Mets were bad. And unless we dilute the talent further, then allow some hideous selections by in-

ept management, we may never see a team this bad again. Hot Rod Kanehl, Marv Throneberry, Charlie Neal, we need you.

Win Some, Lose More

The Most Pitcher Losses in a Season

	Games Lost
1. John Coleman, 1883	48
2. Will White, 1880	42
3. Larry McKeon, 1884	41
4. George Bradley, 1879	40
4. Jim McCormick, 1879	40
6. Pud Galvin, 1880	37
6. George Cobb, 1892	37
6. Kid Corsey, 1891	37
6. Henry Porter, 1888	37
10. Stump Weidman, 1886	36

—From Joseph Reichler, ed., *Baseball Encyclopaedia*, 6th ed., Macmillan, New York, 1985.

No Relief in Sight

The Most Relief Losses in a Season

	Games Lost
1. Gene Garber, 1979	16
2. Darold Knowles, 1970	14
2. Mike Marshall, 1975, 1979	14
2. John Hiller, 1974	14
6. Rollie Fingers, 1978	13
6. Skip Lockwood, 1978	13
6. Wilbur Wood, 1970	13

—From Joseph Reichler, ed., *Baseball Encyclopaedia*, 6th ed., Macmillan, New York, 1985.

As Bad As a Hit (Part I)

The Most Walks Allowed in a Career

		Walks
1.	Nolan Ryan*	2355
2.	Steve Carlton*	1830
3.	Phil Niekro*	1803
4.	Early Wynn	1775
5.	Bob Feller	1764
6.	Bobo Newsom	1732
7.	Amos Rusie	1716
8.	Gus Weyhing	1566
9.	Red Ruffing	1541
10.	Bump Hadley	1442

*Figures through the 1987 season, when these pitchers were still actively walking people.

—From Joseph Reichler, ed., *Baseball Encyclopaedia*, 6th ed., Macmillan, New York, 1985. Updated by *The Worst of Everything*.

As Bad As a Hit (Part II)

The Most Walks Allowed in a Season

		Walks
1.	Amos Rusie, 1893	218
2.	Cy Seymour, 1898	213
3.	Bob Feller, 1938	208
4.	Nolan Ryan, 1977	204
5.	Nolan Ryan, 1974	202
6.	Amos Rusie, 1894	200
7.	Bob Feller, 1941	194
8.	Bobo Newsom, 1938	192
9.	Ted Breitenstein, 1894	191
10.	Tony Mullane, 1893	189

—From Joseph Reichler, ed., *Baseball Encyclopaedia*, 6th ed., Macmillan, New York, 1985.

Special Ks (Part I)

The Most Batter Strikeouts in a Career

		Ks
1.	Reggie Jackson	2597
2.	Willie Stargell	1936
3.	Tony Perez	1845
4.	Bobby Bonds	1757
5.	Lou Brock	1730
6.	Mickey Mantle	1710
7.	Harmon Killebrew	1699
8.	Dave Kingman	1576
9.	Willie Mays	1570
10.	Dick Allen	1556

—From Joseph Reichler, ed., *Baseball Encyclopaedia*, 6th ed., Macmillan, New York, 1985. Updated by *The Worst of Everything* through 1987.

Special Ks (Part II)

The Most Batter Strikeouts in a Season

		Ks
1.	Bobby Bonds, 1970	189
1.	Bobby Bonds, 1969	187
3.	Rob Deer, 1987	186
4.	Pete Incaviglia, 1986	185
5.	Dave Schmidt, 1975	180
6.	Rob Deer, 1986	179
7.	Jose Canseco, 1986	175
7.	Vern Nicholson, 1963	175
7.	Gorman Thomas, 1979	175
10.	Jim Presley, 1986	172

—From Joseph Reichler, ed., *Baseball Encyclopaedia*, 6th ed., Macmillan, New York, 1985. Updated by *The Worst of Everything* through 1987.

Worsts in Professional Basketball

Eat to Lose

The Worst Bodies in Basketball, According to
Bob Ryan

1. REX MORGAN, EX-BOSTON CELTIC GUARD—He lived for the west coast road trips and couldn't say no to any social appointment. That didn't help his body, which had no definition to begin with. He looked like a guy on a college dorm team.

2. DON ADAMS, EX-HOUSTON ROCKET CENTER—Big belly and gut and not much hair. He looked like he should be cleaning up at a racetrack.

3. KEVIN MCHALE, BOSTON CELTIC FORWARD-CENTER —His ex-teammate Mychael Thompson characterized him best: "When I met him, all I could think of was Herman Munster."

4. AL TUCKER, EX-NEW YORK KNICK FORWARD—He could have been captain of the Bangladesh All-Stars.

5. LOUIS ORR, NEW YORK KNICKS FORWARD—Same as above. He reminds me of Olive Oyl.

6. GEOFF CROMPTON—6'11, 300-pounder, and ex-Milwaukee Buck center who can't keep his weight down. He should be weighed on a meat scale.

7. JOE "JELLY BEAN" BRYANT, EX-PHILADELPHIA 76ER, EX-SAN DIEGO CLIPPER—A 6'9" fat man convinced he was a guard, he came into the league looking like Al Tucker and ate his way right out.

—Special to *The Worst of Everything* from Bob Ryan, columnist for the *Boston Globe* and one of the nation's leading basketball writers.

One will note the absence of Manute Bol, all 7 $\frac{1}{2}$ feet worth of drinking straw. Mr. Ryan, this list notwithstanding, is a kind man. No sense belaboring the obvious.

Dribble from the Mouth

The Worst Head Cases in Basketball, According to Bob Ryan

1. JOE "JELLY BEAN" BRYANT—The quintessential head and body case. He may be the only player who looked upon the NBA season as a warm-up for the Baker League (Philadelphia's summer playground league). He uttered the great basketball quote of the 1980s in explaining why he was cut by an NBA team: "I guess they weren't ready for a Magic Johnson type." When Bryant looked in the mirror, he saw something no one else did.

2. JOHN BRISKER—A great head case with talent. He came to the Seattle Supersonics as an ABA star and couldn't get with the program. Bill Russell (then the Sonics coach) couldn't stand him.

3. ERIC MONEY—The quintessential product of the hardship draft. He came to the NBA at 19, and nobody could tell him anything. He was gone by the time he was 24.

4. SYDNEY WICKS—One of the most effective college forwards ever. He was a UCLA product, so everyone figured he was the usual John Wooden team player, but as soon as he got to Portland he got into a one-upmanship contest with Geoff Petrie, a high-scoring guard. There's a story that John Wooden won't verify, but that I believe—that Wooden considered Wicks the worst character ever to play for UCLA.

—Special to *The Worst of Everything* from Bob Ryan, columnist for the *Boston Globe* and one of the nation's leading basketball writers.

It Was a Charge, Ref

The Most Personal Fouls

...IN A QUARTER

	Fouls
1. Jim Krebs, Los Angeles at Boston, April 21, 1963	5
1. Brian Winters, Milwaukee at Phiadelphia, April 10, 1981	5
1. Mark West, Dallas at Los Angeles, April 28, 1984	5

...IN A GAME

1. Jack Toomay, Baltimore at New York, March 26, 1949 (overtime)	8
2. Al Cervi, Syracuse at Boston, March 21, 1953 (overtime)	7

...IN A SEASON

1. Darryl Dawkins, Philadelphia, 1983–1984	387
2. Darryl Dawkins, Philadelphia, 1982–1983	379
3. Steve Johnson, Kansas City, 1981–1982	372

...IN A CAREER

1. Kareem Abdul-Jabbar*	4245
2. Elvin Hayes	4193
3. Hal Greer	3855
4. Dolph Schayes	3664
5. Walt Bellamy	3536
6. Bailey Howell	3498
7. Sam Lacey	3473
8. Bill Bridges	3375

| 9. Len Wilkens | 3285 |
| 10. John Havlicek | 3281 |

*Still active, still fouling. Statistics as of 1986–87 season.

———
—All the above statistics are from the *Sporting News Official NBA Guide,* 1987–1988.

You're In, You're Out

The Fastest Disqualifications

	Min Played
1. Dick Farley, Syracuse at St. Louis, March 12, 1956	5
2. Bill Bridges, St. Louis at New York, October 29, 1963	6
2. Johnny Green, Baltimore at San Francisco, October 28, 1966	6
2. Jim Barnes, Los Angeles at Philadelphia, December 2, 1966	6
2. Leonard Gray, Washington at Philadelphia, April 9, 1977	6
2. Chris Engler, Golden State at Utah, March 5, 1983	6

A Noncontact Game

The Most Disqualifications, Both Teams, in a Game

	DQs
1. Syracuse (8) at Baltimore (5), November 15, 1952	13
2. Syracuse (6) at Boston (5), December 26, 1950	11

Designated Hitter (Part I)

The Most Disqualifications in a Season

1. Don Meneke, Fort Worth, 1952–1953	26
2. Steve Johnson, Kansas City, 1981–1982	25
3. Darryl Dawkins, Philadelphia, 1982–1983	23

Designated Hitter (Part II)

The Most Disqualifications in a Career

1. Vern Mikkelsen	127
2. Walter Dukes	121
3. Charlie Share	105

Designated Hitter (Part III)

The Highest Percentages of Games Disqualified

	% Games
1. Walter Dukes	21.88
2. Vern Mikkelsen	18.17
3. Charlie Share	17.62

—All of the above statistics are from *Sporting News Official NBA Guide*, 1987–88.

You Take It

The Most Turnovers

...IN A CAREER

	Turnovers
1. Moses Malone*	2711
2. Reggie Theus*	2587
3. Julius Irving	2323

---

*Still active, still turning 'em over. Statistics through 1986–1987 season.

...IN A SEASON

1. Artis Gilmore, 1977–1978	366
2. Kevin Porter, 1977–1978	360
3. Michael Ray Richardson, 1979–1980	359

...IN A GAME, INDIVIDUAL

1. John Drew, Atlanta at New Jersey, March 1, 1978	14
2. Kevin Porter, New Jersey at Philadelphia, November 9, 1977; Detroit at Philadelphia, February 7, 1979	12
2. Artis Gilmore, Chicago at Atlanta, January 31, 1978	12
2. Maurice Lucas, New Jersey at Phoenix, November 25, 1978	12
2. Moses Malone, Houston at Phoenix, February 6, 1980	12

...IN A GAME, TEAM

1. Los Angeles vs. Seattle, February 15, 1974	43
2. New Jersey vs. Detroit, November 16, 1980	41

1. Denver, 1976–1977	24.5
2. Buffalo, 1972–1973	24.4
3. Philadelphia, 1976–1977	23.4

You Keep It

The Fewest Steals per Game in a Season

	Steals
1. Boston, 1976–1977	6.20
2. Washington, 1979–1980	6.46
3. Los Angeles Clippers, 1984–1985	6.51

You Dribble, You Shoot

The Fewest Assists per Game in a Season

	Assists
1. Minneapolis, 1956–1957	16.6
2. New York Nets, 1976–1977	17.3
3. Detroit, 1957–1958	17.6

You Shoot, You Miss (Part I)

The Worst Field Goal Percentages in a Season

	FG %
1. Milwaukee, 1954–1955	.3620
2. Syracuse, 1956–1957	.3688
3. Rochester, 1956–1957	.3695

You Shoot, You Miss (Part II)

The Worst Field Goal Percentages in a Game

1. Milwaukee vs. Minneapolis,
   November 6, 1954   .229
2. New York vs. Milwaukee,
   December 31, 1954   .235
3. Cleveland vs. San Francisco,
   November 10, 1970   .238

—All the above statistics are from the *Sporting News Official NBA Record Book,* 1986.

Get 'em Next Season

The Worst Winning Percentages in a Season

	%age (Record)
1. Philadelphia, 1972–1973	.110 (9–73)
2. Providence, 1947–1948	.125 (6–42)
3. Houston, 1982–1983	.171 (14–68)

Get 'em Next Game

The Most Consecutive Games Lost

	Consecutive Losses
1. Cleveland, 1982	24
2. Detroit, 1980	21
3. Philadelphia, 1973	20
4. Philadelphia, 1972	19
4. San Diego, 1982	19

Home Court Disadvantage

The Most Consecutive Home Games Lost

	Consecutive Losses
1. Cleveland, 1982	15
2. Philadelphia, 1972	13
2. Detroit, 1980	13

Biting the Road Apple

The Most Consecutive Road Games Lost

1. Baltimore, 1953–1954	32
2. San Diego, 1983	29
3. New Orleans, 1974–1975	28
3. Atlanta, 1976	28
3. Indiana, 1983	28

All the above statistics are from the *Sporting News Official NBA Record Book,* 1986.

WORSTS IN COLLEGE BASKETBALL

Dirty Women (Part I)

*The Most Personal Fouls per Game
in a Season (NCAA, Division 1)*

	Fpg
Loyola, Maryland, 1982 (942 in 27 games)	34.9

Dirty Women (Part II)

The Most Personal Fouls in a Game, Team

	Fouls
Nevada-Reno (vs. San Diego State), January 3, 1984	40
Hardin-Simmons (vs. Texas Lutheran), January 24, 1984	40

Boring Women

The Worst Offensive Performance in a Game, Both Teams

	Pts
Virginia (38) vs. San Diego State (34), December 29, 1981	72

Boring Guys (Part I)

The Most Consecutive Defeats

	Consecutive losses
The Citadel, from January 16, 1954, to December 12, 1955	37

Boring Guys (Part II)

The Most Defeats in a Season

	Record
Washington State, 1953	3–27
University of Pacific, 1984	3–27
U.S. International, 1985	1–27

Boring Guys (Part III)

The Fewest Points Scored in a Game

	Total Pts
Tennessee (11) vs. Temple (6), December 15, 1973	17

Records kept since 1937.

Boring Guys (Part IV)

The Biggest Wipeout

Louisiana State 124, Southwestern
Tennessee 33, December 8, 1952

Dirty Men (Part I)

The Most Personal Fouls in a Season, Team

	Fouls
Houston, 1977 (37 games)	849

Dirty Men (Part II)

The Most Personal Fouls per Game, Team

	Fpg
Indiana, 1952 (644 in 22 games)	29.3

Dirty Men (Part III)

The Most Personal Fouls in a Game, Team

Total Fouls

Arizona (vs. Northern Arizona),   50
  January 26, 1953

Dirty Men (Part IV)

The Most Players Disqualified in a Game

DQs

St. Joseph's (PA) (vs. Xavier),   8
  January 10, 1976

All the above statistics are from the 1986 NCAA Basketball Record Book.

WORSTS IN PROFESSIONAL FOOTBALL

In No Rush (Part I)

The Fewest Sacks in a Season

	Sacks
1. Baltimore, 1982	11
2. Buffalo, 1982	12
3. Baltimore, 1981	13

In No Rush (Part II)

The Fewest Yards Lost by Opponents
Attempting to Pass, in a Season

	Yds Lost, Opponent
1. Green Bay, 1956	75
2. New York Bulldogs, 1949	77
3. Green Bay, 1958	78

I Don't Want It

The Fewest Opponents' Fumbles
Recovered in a Season

	Recoveries
1. Los Angeles, 1974	3
2. Philadelphia, 1944	4
2. San Francisco, 1982	4
4. Baltimore, 1982	5

Take It, It's Mine

The Most Turnovers in a Season

	Turnovers
1. San Francisco, 1978	63
2. Chicago Bears, 1947	58
2. Pittsburgh, 1950	58
2. New York Giants, 1983	58
5. Green Bay, 1950	57
5. Houston, 1962, 1963	57
5. Pittsburgh, 1965	57

Take It, It's Mine (Part II)

The Most Turnovers in a Game

	Turnovers
1. Detroit vs. Chicago Bears, November 22, 1942	12
1. Chicago Cardinals vs. Philadelphia, September 24, 1950	12
1. Pittsburgh vs. Philadelphia, December 12, 1965	12

Flag Football (Part I)

The Most Penalties in a Game

	Penalties
1. Brooklyn vs. Green Bay, September 17, 1944	22
1. Chicago Bears vs. Philadelphia, November 26, 1944	22
3. Cleveland vs. Chicago Bears, November 25, 1951	21
4. Tampa Bay vs. Seattle, October 17, 1976	20

Flag Football (Part II)

The Most Years Leading the League in the Most Penalties

	Years
1. Chicago Bears	16
2. Oakland/Los Angeles Raiders	7
3. Los Angeles Rams	6

Flag Football (Part III)

The Most Yards Penalized in a Season

	Yds Lost
1. Oakland, 1969	1274
2. Baltimore, 1979	1239
3. Los Angeles Raiders, 1984	1209

C'mon In

The Most Times Sacked in a Season

	Times Sacked
1. Atlanta, 1968	70
2. Dallas, 1964	68
3. Detroit, 1976	67
4. Atlanta, 1984	67

—All the above statistics are from the *NFL Record & Fact Book*, 1986; courtesy of Sports Features Syndicate, Inc.

I Don't Want It, You Can Have It

The Worst Football Fumblers

...PER CAREER

	Fumbles
1. Roman Gabriel, Los Angeles, 1962–1972; Philadelphia, 1973–1977	105
2. Johnny Unitas, Baltimore, 1956–1972; San Diego, 1973	95
3. Franco Harris, Pittsburgh, 1972–1983; Seattle, 1984	90

4. Len Dawson, Pittsburgh, 1957–1959;
   Cleveland, 1960–1961; Dallas Texans, 1962;
   Kansas City, 1963–1975   84

...PER SEASON

1. Dan Pastorini, Houston, 1973   17
2. Don Meredith, Dallas, 1964   16
3. Paul Christman, Chicago
   Cardinals, 1946   15
3. Sammy Baugh, Washington, 1947   15
3. Sam Etcheverry, St. Louis, 1961   15
3. Len Dawson, Kansas City, 1964   15
3. Terry Metcalf, St. Louis, 1976   15
3. Steve DeBerg, Tampa Bay, 1985   15

...PER GAME

1. Len Dawson, Kansas City vs.
   San Diego, November 15, 1964   7
2. Sam Etcheverry, St. Louis vs. New
   York Giants, September 17, 1961   6
3. Paul Christman, Chicago Cardinals
   vs. Green Bay, November 10, 1946   5
3. Charlie Conerly, New York Giants
   vs. San Francisco, December 1, 1957   5
3. Jack Kemp, Buffalo vs. Houston,
   October 29, 1967   5
3. Roman Gabriel, Philadelphia vs.
   Oakland, November 21, 1976   5

—All the above statistics are from the NFL public relations department, 1986.

Everyone Got in the Act

The Most Fumbles by a Team in a Season

	Fumbles
1. Chicago Bears, 1938	56
1. San Francisco 49ers, 1978	56

Take the Redskins +74

The Worst Loss in an NFL Game

Chicago Bears 73, Washington Redskins 0;
December 8, 1940 (NFL Championship)

A Different Kind of Perfect

The Worst Season in NFL History

	Record
Tampa Bay Buccaneers, 1976	0–14

All the above statistics are from the *NRL Record & Fact Book*, 1986; courtesy of Sports Features Syndicate, Inc.

The Refrigerator Belongs in the Kitchen

The 5 Worst Football Plays and Strategies, According to Paul Zimmerman

1. Punts into the middle of the end zone

2. Quarterback kneeldowns

3. Draw plays on 3rd and 25

4. Final-minute time-outs when down by 2 touchdowns or
more

5. Prevent defenses

_____

—Special to *The Worst of Everything* from Paul Zimmerman, football writer
for *Sports Illustrated*.

*Yes, this is the same guy who's the wine expert. These are,
then, the plays that drive him to drink. I'd add, running plays
suggested by Richard Nixon or speeches made by Ron "the
Gipper" Reagan.*

WORSTS IN PROFESSIONAL
ICE HOCKEY

Get 'em Next Year

The Most Losses in a Season

	Losses
1. Washington Capitals, 1974–1975	67
2. New York Islanders, 1972–1973	60
3. Washington Capitals, 1975–1976	59

Get 'em Next Game

The Longest Winless Streaks in a Season

	Consecutive Losses
1. Winnipeg Jets, 1980	30
2. Kansas City Scouts, 1976	27
3. Washington Capitals, 1975–1976	25

Home Ice Disadvantage

The Most Losses at Home in a Season

1.	Pittsburgh Penguins, 1983–1984	29
2.	Washington Capitals, 1974–1975	28
2.	New Jersey Devils, 1983–1984	28
4.	Los Angeles Kings, 1985–1986	27
5.	Washington Capitals, 1975–1976	26
6.	New York Islanders, 1972–1973	25
6.	Winnipeg Jets, 1980–1981	25

Biting the Road Apple

The Fewest Road Wins in a Season

		Road Record
1.	Toronto Arenas, 1918–1919	0–9
1.	Quebec Bulldogs, 1919–1920	0–12
1.	Pittsburgh Pirates, 1929–1930	0–22
2.	Hamilton Tigers, 1921–1922	1–12
2.	Toronto St. Patricks, 1925–1926	1–18
2.	Philadelphia Quakers, 1930–1931	1–22
2.	New York Americans, 1940–1941	1–24
2.	Washington Capitals, 1974–1975	1–40

—All the above statistics are from the *1985 Official Guide & Record Book*, National Hockey League.

Don't Shoot (Part I)

The Fewest Goals Scored in a Season

		Goals
1.	Chicago Black Hawks, 1928–1929 (44 games)	33
2.	Montreal Maroons, 1924–1925 (30 games)	45

3. Pittsburgh Pirates, 1928–1929   46
   (44 games)

—All the above statistics are from the *1985 Official Guide & Record Book,*
National Hockey League.

Don't Shoot (Part II)

The Most Goals Scored against a Team in a Season

	Goals
1. Washington Capitals, 1974–1975	446
2. Detroit Redwings, 1985–1986	415
3. Hartford Whalers, 1982–1983	403
4. Vancouver Canucks, 1984–1985	401
5. Winnipeg Jets, 1980–1981	400

—All the above statistics are from the *1987 Official Guide & Record Book,*
National Hockey League.

The Man in the Glass Booth (Part I)

The Most Penalty Minutes Assessed in a Game

	Penalty Min
1. Randy Holt, Los Angeles Kings, March 11, 1979, at Philadelphia (1 minor, 3 majors, two 10-minute misconducts, 3 game misconducts)	67
2. Frank Bathe, Philadelphia Flyers, March 11, 1979, at Philadelphia (3 majors, two 10-minute misconducts, 2 game misconducts)	55
3. Russ Anderson, Pittsburgh Penguins, January 19, 1980, at Pittsburgh (3 minors, 3 majors, 3 game misconducts)	51

The Man in the Glass Booth (part II)

The Most Penalty Minutes Assessed in a Season

	Penalty Min
1. Dave Schultz, Philadelphia Flyers, 1974–1975	472
2. Paul Baxter, Pittsburgh Penguins, 1981–1982	407
3. Dave Schultz, Los Angeles and Pittsburgh, 1977–1978	405

—All the above statistics are from the *1987 Official Guide & Record Book*, National Hockey League.

Two Minutes for Anything

The All-Time Regular-Season Penalty-Minute Leaders

	Penalty Min
1. Dave Williams	3873
2. Dave Schultz	2294
3. Bryan Watson	2212
4. Willi Plett	2402
5. Terry O'Reilly	2095
6. Phil Russell	2038
7. Andre Dupont	1986
8. Chris Nolan	1965
9. Gary Howatt	1836
10. Carol Vadnais	1813

—All the above statistics are from the *1987 Official Guide & Record Book*, National Hockey League.

Goon Squads

The Dirtiest Teams

	Penalty Min
1. Philadelphia Flyers, 1980–1981	2621
2. Philadelphia Flyers, 1981–1982	2493
3. Pittsburgh Penguins, 1981–1982	2210

A Hockey Game Never Broke Out

The Dirtiest Game Ever Played

In a game between the Minnesota North Stars and the Boston Bruins at Boston on February 26, 1981, there were 84 penalties called, for a total of 406 minutes. Minnesota received 198 minors, 13 majors, four 10-minute misconducts, and 7 game misconducts for a total of 42 penalties and 211 minutes. Boston received 20 minors, 13 majors, three 10-minute misconducts, and 6 game misconducts for a total of 42 penalties and 195 minutes. The totals constitute the most penalty minutes and penalties ever assessed in 1 game.

—All the above statistics are from the *1987 Official Guide & Record Book,* National Hockey League.

What mystifies me about hockey is how these guys who all come from the same stretch of frozen tundra, see each other every other week, and play for the same teams at some point in their careers still manage to work up the animosity to smack each other around with such abandon. The fact that they have no teeth left to lose may remove a few inhibitions, but the rest is a mystery—one well worth ignoring.

WORSTS IN PROFESSIONAL BOWLING

Clobbered

The Biggest Margin of Victory in a Match Play Tournament Final*

Larry Laub, 290
Mark Estes, 118

*Waukegan, IL, August 27, 1975; 172 pins.

Pins and Needles

The Lowest-Scoring TV Championship Game*

Dennis Jacques, 157
Sam Zurich, 156

*Windsor, Ontario, August 23, 1983.

—From the Professional Bowling Association; courtesy of Sports Features Syndicate, Inc.

We can't do much about bowling—would you believe this is America's favorite sport—and you won't catch us watching it, so the least we can do is keep the listings brief. What exactly did happen to Mark Estes, though? Did he drop a ball on his foot? His head? Was he overcome by the pressure of playing for pocket change before 30 or more relatives? By remorse for a lane violation? Or by the sheer ennui that overcomes us at the mere thought of tenpin tourneys?

WORSTS IN PROFESSIONAL BOXING

Shadow Boxers

The 6 Worst Boxing Champions of the 1980s, According to Steve Marantz

1. Alfonzo Ratliff, 195 lb, lost to Bernard Benton.

2. Bernard Benton, 195 lb, barely beat Alfonzo Ratliff.

3. Tadashi Mihara, 154 lb, won the vacant junior middle-weight title in a match against Rocky Fratto.

4. Tony Tubbs, heavyweight, fat and reluctant

4. Greg Page, heavyweight, fat and reluctant

4. Michael Dokes, heavyweight, fat and reluctant

—Special to *The Worst of Everything* from Steven Marantz, boxing columnist for the *Boston Globe*.

Thanks for the above go to sleazy egomaniacs Don King and Bob Arum for creating "opportunities" for these less-than-deserving puglists, and to the WBC, WBA, and IBF frauds who create championships to create challengers to create cash opportunities. Let Arum and King go 15, then give the winner all the belts to distribute.

WORSTS IN PROFESSIONAL GOLF

Right Place, Wrong Time

The Lowest Earnings by a Leading PGA Money Winner

Paul Runyan, 1934, $6767

—From *Golf Digest Almanac*; courtesy of Sports Features Syndicate, Inc.

Whatever I said about bowling goes for golf in spades. Why do all golfers buy their leisure clothes off the same rack at Anderson-Little? Why do they need to think over shots they've hit a thousand times before? Practice their swings? Keep quiet and make the rest of us do the same? Why can't they carry their own clubs? What this game needs is defense—people trying to swat down shots, block swings, move the hole in midputt. Now we're talking sport.

WORSTS IN PROFESSIONAL TENNIS

All's Fair in Love Sets

The 9 Worst Tennis Tantrums, According
to Bud Collins

1. Ilie Nastase mooned a referee at a 1976 Palm Springs tournament.

2. Ilie Nastase's bickering and stalling at the 1975 Stockholm Masters tournament so provoked opponent Arthur Ashe that Ashe walked off the court in disgust though leading 4–1 in the third set. Referee Horst Klosterkemper then disqualified Nastase, so the match had 2 losers.

3. American Clark Graebner was so incensed by Ilie Nastase's antics in a 1972 London match that he charged the net and grabbed Nastase, threatening to pummel him. Nastase was so frightened he forfeited.

4. American Cliff Ritchie became so angry at line calls during a 1972 Houston match that he ripped up the lines taped and nailed to the court.

5. Ilie Nastase concluded a 1976 Forest Hills shouting match with German opponent Hans Pohmann by spitting at him.

6. John McEnroe called referee Fred Hoiles everything in the book, and also called Wimbledon "the pits" in the first round of the 1981 tournament, then went on to win the All-England Tennis Championship.

7. In a Stockholm match in 1984, John McEnroe in a rage over calls knocked all the glasses and bottles off a courtside table.

8. Mark Edmondson of Australia banged an umpire's chair at Wimbledon in 1981.

9. Billie Jean King threw her racquet at and hit umpire Gene Parker's chair in a 1982 Boston Virginia Slims tournament match.

—Special to *The Worst of Everything* from Bud Collins, NBC tennis commentator and columnist for the *Boston Globe*.

The most appealing of all to me is #3. Why does one player watch while the other cavorts? Why do the umpires put up with such prima donna behavior when players in other sports get penalized, ejected for far less? Why am I asking all these questions? The point is, the more tantrums the better, and instead of discouraging them in tennis we should encourage athletes in other sports to behave the same way. Look how boring tennis is now that Nastase is gone and McEnroe is a cool papa.

CLIMATE AND ENVIRONMENTAL WORSTS

What do African violets, bumblebee bats, the people of Manila, and you (if you've been bitten by a taipan) have in common? You are all in grave jeopardy because of your environment. No one's chuckling in Troy, NY, or in Alabama, Ontario, or Kentucky for reasons you will discover herein—or if you live and breathe in those places, in your next pulmonary x-ray.

These are among the places we've done our level best to make uninhabitable. But there are many that had a head start. Don't take your galoshes to Cairo, but don't step out in Hong Kong without them. Galveston is nature's Turkish bath, and Biloxi is its torture chamber. Don't go to Syracuse in the winter, Phoenix in the summer, or Grand Forks ever, if you value comfort.

Any one of these places could make you sick. And don't go to Glens Falls to get better. Then again, if we all knew what was good for us, how did we ever get ourselves in such a fix?

Hot Enough for You, Bub?

The 10 Hottest Major Cities on Earth

		Ave Ann Temp, °F
1.	Bangkok	83.1
1.	Manila	83.1
3.	Jidda	81.9
4.	Bombay	81.1
5.	Singapore	80.6
6.	Lagos	80.2
7.	Manama	79.5
8.	Nairobi	79.2
9.	Tel Aviv	78.6
10.	Jakarta	78.3

—From John T. Marlin, Immanuel Ness, and Stephen T. Collins, *Book of World City Rankings*, Free Press, New York, 1986.

To be found here and on the following pages are what should be compelling specific reasons not to live in or visit any of the cities mentioned. The statistics presented, thorough as they are, fail, however, to factor in those habitations where a single day's weather brings a variety of tortures dependent on season and cruel vagary of nature. As Mark Twain said about New England, "If you don't like the weather, wait a minute," or some such. What he surely meant to imply was that in a minute it will change to something else equally disagreeable.

Cold Enough for You, Bub?

The 10 Coldest Major Cities on Earth

		Ave Ann Temp, °F
1.	Winnipeg	36.5
2.	Edmonton	36.9
3.	Calgary	39.0
4.	Leningrad	39.6
5.	Moscow	39.9
6.	Helsinki	40.6
7.	Ottawa	42.3
8.	Oslo	42.6
9.	Stockholm	43.9
10.	Montreal	44.4

—From John T. Marlin, Immanuel Ness, and Stephen T. Collins, *Book of World City Rankings,* Free Press, New York, 1986.

You Came to Casablanca for the Waters?

The 10 Driest Major Cities on Earth

		Ave Ann Rainfall, in
1.	Cairo	0.9
2.	Manama	3.0

2. Jidda	3.0
4. Phoenix	7.0
5. San Diego	9.4
6. Ankara	13.5
7. Los Angeles	14.5
8. Santiago	15.0
9. Athens	15.8
10. Calgary	16.7

—From John T. Marlin, Immanuel Ness, and Stephen T. Collins, *Book of World City Rankings*, Free Press, New York, 1986.

Who'll Stop the Rain?

The 11 Wettest Major Cities on Earth

	Ave Ann Rainfall, in
1. Hong Kong	85.1
2. Taipei	82.7
3. Manila	81.1
4. Bombay	71.5
5. Jakarta	70.8
6. Lagos	64.0
7. Yokohama	62.4
8. Tokyo	61.5
9. Nagoya	60.9
10. Kyoto	57.4
10. Vancouver	57.4

—From John T. Marlin, Immanuel Ness, and Stephen T. Collins, *Book of World City Rankings*, Free Press, New York, 1986.

Don't Go Out Tonight

The 20 U.S Metropolitan Areas with the Worst Weather*

1. Grand Forks, ND

2. Fargo-Moorhead, ND, MN

3. Bismarck, ND

4. Duluth, MN

5. St. Cloud, MN

6. Anchorage, AK

7. McAllen-Edinburg-Mission, TX

8. Eau Claire, WI

9. Sioux Falls, SD

10. Minneapolis–St. Paul, MN, WI

11. Lakeland–Winter Haven, FL

12. Wausau, WI

13. Rochester, NY

14. Ocala, FL

15. Victoria, TX

16. Dothan, AL

17. Fort Myers, FL

18. Waterloo–Cedar Falls, IA

19. La Crosse, WI

20. Corpus Christi, TX

—From Richard Boyer and David Savageau, *Places Rated Almanac*, Rand McNally, Chicago, 1985.

*Metropolitan areas rated worst for mildness on 6 combined factors: very hot and very cold months, seasonal temperature variation, heating- and cooling-degree days, freezing days, zero-degree days, and 90-degree days.

Colder Than a Witch's Heart

The 10 Worst U.S. Cities for Subfreezing Days

		Days/Yr
1.	Helena, MT	189
1.	Reno, NV	189
3.	Casper, WY	186
4.	Fargo, ND	181
5.	Cheyenne, WY	172
6.	Sioux Falls, SD	171
7.	Madison, WI	164
8.	Burlington, VT	163
9.	Colorado Springs, CO	162
10.	Portland, ME	160

—From *199 American Cities Compared,* Information Publications, Burlington, VT, 1984 (U.S. Dept. of Commerce).

Water Torture

The 10 Worst U.S. Cities for Days of Precipitation per Year

		Days/Yr
1.	Juneau, AK	220
2.	Syracuse, NY	166
3.	Youngstown, OH	162
3.	Erie, PA	162
3.	Olympia, WA	162
6.	Cleveland, OH	155
7.	Rochester, NY	154
8.	Burlington, VT	153
8.	Seattle, WA	153
10.	Portland, OR	152

—From *199 American Cities Compared,* Information Publications, Burlington, VT, 1984 (U.S. Dept. of Commerce).

Hot Time, Summer in the City

The 10 Worst U.S. Cities for 90+ Degree Days

	Days/Yr
1. Phoenix, AZ	139
2. Las Vegas, NV	133
3. San Antonio, TX	111
4. Bakersfield, CA	108
5. Fresno, CA	108
6. Orlando, FL	107
7. El Paso, TX	105
7. Waco, TX	105
9. Austin, TX	103
10. Corpus Christi, TX	101

—From *199 American Cities Compared,* Information Publications, Burlington, VT, 1984 (U.S. Dept. of Commerce).

Shovel off to Buffalo

The 10 U.S. Metropolitan Areas with the Most Annual Snowfall

	In, Ave
1. Syracuse, NY	109
2. Bangor, ME	97
3. Buffalo, NY	90
4. Binghamton, NY	86
5. Burlington, VT	79
6. Duluth, MN, WI	78
7. Casper, WY	77
7. Grand Rapids, MI	77
9. Portland, ME	74
10. Albany-Schenectady-Troy, NY	71

—From Richard Boyer and David Savageau, *Places Rated Almanac,* Rand McNally, Chicago, 1985.

Worst Places to Sell Your Umbrella

The 7 U.S. Metropolitan Areas with the Lowest Relative Humidity

	%, Ave
1. Las Vegas, NV	29
2. Phoenix, AZ	36
3. Tucson, AZ	38
4. El Paso, TX	39
5. Albuquerque, NM	43
6. Colorado Springs, CO	49
7. Reno, NV	50

—From Richard Boyer and David Savageau, *Places Rated Almanac*, Rand McNally, Chicago, 1985.

Can't Sell Your Humidifier?

The 8 U.S. Metropolitan Areas with the Highest Relative Humidity

	%, Ave
1. Galveston–Texas City, TX	78
2. Alexandria, LA	77
2. Asheville, NC	77
2. Biloxi-Gulfport, MS	77
2. Corpus Christi, TX	77
2. Eugene-Springfield, OR	77
2. Houston, TX	77
2. New Orleans, LA	77

—From Richard Boyer and David Savageau, *Places Rated Almanac*, Rand McNally, Chicago, 1985.

My Corns Hurt

The 11 U.S. Metropolitan Areas
with the Most Storm Days

		# of Days
1.	Biloxi-Gulfport, MS	94
2.	Fort Myers, FL	93
3.	Tampa–St. Petersburg–Clearwater, FL	88
4.	Tallahassee, FL	86
5.	Orlando, FL	81
6.	Mobile, AL	80
7.	Miami-Hialeah, FL	75
8.	Galveston–Texas City, TX	70
9.	Alexandria, LA	69
9.	Houston, TX	69
11.	New Orleans, LA	68

—From Richard Boyer and David Savageau, *Places Rated Almanac*, Rand McNally, Chicago, 1985.

Unhealthy, Unwealthy

The 20 Worst U.S. Metropolitan Areas for
Health Care and Environment*

1. Glens Falls, NY

2. Brownsville-Harlingen, TX

3. Midland, TX

4. Provo-Orem, UT

5. Panama City, FL

6. Visalia-Tulare-Porterville, CA

7. Yuba City, CA

8. St. Joseph, MO

9. San Angelo, TX

10. Abilene, TX

11. Bellingham, WA

12. Chico, CA

13. Medford, OR

14. Victoria, TX

15. Redding, CA

16. Richland-Kennewick-Pasco, WA

17. Mansfield, OH

18. Bremerton, WA

19. Lake Charles, LA

20. Yakima, WA

*Criteria used are physicians per 100,000 population, teaching hospitals, medical schools, cardiac rehabilitation centers, comprehensive cancer treatment centers, hospices, insurance/hospitalization costs, fluoridation of drinking water, and air pollution.

—From Richard Boyer and David Savageau, *Places Rated Almanac,* Rand McNally, Chicago, 1985.

They have or had, as I recall, a grand prix race in Glens Falls. If you live there it might be a good idea to enter, especially if you have no racing experience. At least you'll go fast, one way or the other.

Don't Breathe if You Want to Live

*The 17 Worst U.S. Metropolitan Areas for Air Pollution**

1. Albuquerque, NM

2. Anaheim–Santa Ana, CA

3. Baltimore, MD

4. Boise, ID

5. Chicago, IL

6. Denver, CO

7. Detroit, MI

8. El Paso, TX

9. Fresno, CA

10. Jersey City, NJ

11. Los Angeles–Long Beach, CA

12. Minneapolis–St. Paul, MN, WI

13. Nashville, TN

14. Phoenix, AZ

15. Riverside–San Bernardino, CA

16. Steubenville-Weirton, OH, WV

17. Tucson, WA

*Exceeding limits for 2 or more major pollutants, according to 1983 Environmental Protection Agency standards.

—From Richard Boyer and David Savageau, *Places Rated Almanac*, Rand McNally, Chicago, 1985.

Raindrops Keep Burning through My Head

The 16 U.S. Metropolitan Areas with the Worst Acid Rain*

1. Albany-Schenectady-Troy, NY

2. Atlantic City, NJ

3. Baltimore, MD

4. Duluth, MN, WI

5. Eau Claire, WI

6. Eugene-Springfield, OR

7. Glens Falls, NY

8. Hagerstown, MD

9. Medford, OR

10. Middlesex-Somerset-Hunterdon, NJ

11. Monmouth-Ocean Counties, NJ

12. St. Cloud, MN, WI

13. Salt Lake City–Ogden, UT

14. Trenton, NJ

15. Vineland-Millville-Bridgeton, NJ

16. Wausau, WI

*Areas with present or potential acid rain problems from U.S. Geological Survey, 1984.

—From Richard Boyer and David Savageau, *Places Rated Almanac*, Rand McNally, Chicago, 1985.

Of course, this is a question requiring further study, as President Reagan has so long and often pointed out. Only problem is all the fish and trees will soon be gone from these areas—along with the people, if they sense what's good for them. And the studies will then be that much more difficult to complete. How are we supposed to figure out if the stuff is dangerous if nothing stays alive long enough to test?

Smoke Gets in Your Lungs

North America's 5 Worst Power Plant Polluters

1. Paradise, KY, Tennessee Valley Authority

2. Cumberland, TN, Tennessee Valley Authority

3. Clifty Creek, IN, American Electric Power Company

4. Monroe, MI, Detroit Edison

5. Baldwin, IL, Illinois Power Corporation

*Total sulphur dioxide emissions, 1981. "The total tonnage of sulphur and nitrogen oxides emitted by various smelter and power plants can vary widely from month to month and year to year, depending on the vicissitudes of markets and demand. A list of Worst Polluters can thus serve only as a rough indicator of trouble spots, rather than an exact ranking...."

—From Thomas Pawlick, *A Killing Rain: The Global Threat of Acid Precipitation*, Sierra Club Books, San Francisco, 1984.

Smoke Gets in Your Lungs (Part II)

*North America's 10 Worst Polluters**

	SO_2, Kilotons
1. Inco, Ontario	807.5
2. Noranda Mines, Quebec	537.5
3. TVA, Paradise, KY	418.8
4. Inco, Manitoba	333.5
5. AEP, Munskingum, OH	306.7
6. AEP, Galion, OH	297.5
7. TVA, Cumberland, TN	296.2
8. AEP, Clifty Creek, IN	295.3
9. Illinois Power Corporation, Baldwin, IL	237.2
10. Detroit Edison, Monroe, MI	224.3

*1980 ratings. "The total tonnage of sulphur and nitrogen oxides emitted by various smelter and power plants can vary widely from month to month and year to year, depending on the vicissitudes of markets and demand. A list of Worst Polluters can thus serve only as a rough indicator of trouble spots, rather than an exact ranking...."

—From Thomas Pawlick, *A Killing Rain: the Global Threat of Acid Precipitation*, Sierra Club Books, San Francisco, 1984.

It's Brown, It Smells, and You're Breathing It

The 10 Cities with the Worst Air on Earth

		SO_2,* Mg/μm
1.	Milan	285.9
2.	São Paulo	133.2
3.	Brussels	96.1
4.	Madrid	93.8
5.	Liverpool	90.8
6.	Manila	90.6
7.	Frankfurt	77.6
8.	Glasgow	76.4
9.	Paris	71.1
10.	Bogotá	68.4

*Mean rating

—From John T. Marlin, Immanuel Ness, and Stephen T. Collins, *Book of World City Rankings*, Free Press, New York, 1986.

Former mayor of New York John V. Lindsay used to joke he didn't like to breathe air he couldn't see. Is he spending his retirement in Milan? I still think of that city as a stylish metropolis. But is everyone wearing brown these days? Should we change Veal Milanese to a black gravy? Put tar in Mint Milano cookies? All right, forget it. But bear in mind, this place is more than twice as foul as any other city, and 3 times as foul as all but one other. Plan accordingly. What is Italian for "Can you change my gas mask filter?"

Environment, Shmenvironment

The 12 Worst States for Environmental Effort

1. Alabama

2. Missouri

3. Mississippi

4. Idaho

5. New Mexico

6. Oklahoma

7. New Hampshire

7. Louisiana

9. Texas

9. North Dakota

9. Nevada

9. Nebraska

—From the Conservation Foundation, 1983.

And You Were Worried about Your Pension

The 5 Worst Threats to Life and to Our Future, According to Norman Myers

1. CLIMATIC DISLOCATIONS—The buildup of carbon dioxide and other greenhouse gases in the global atmosphere, the albedo effect, and other disruptions of climatic regimes threaten radical change in our environment.

2. MASS EXTINCTION OF SPECIES—We face the prospect of elimination of one-fifth of all species by the year 2000, and elimination of as many as one-third, conceivably one-half, by the end of the next century. Massive costs will accrue in terms of depleted genetic contributions to agriculture, medicine, industry, and energy.

3. TROPICAL DEFORESTATION—We face the impending demise of the greatest celebration of nature to ever appear on the planet—loss of millions of species, watershed services, and climatic stabilization factors.

4. LOSS OF TOPSOIL—We may lose the greater part of our topsoil by the middle of the next century—at roughly the same time exploitable stocks of petroleum are expected to run out. We shall find ways to get by without petroleum, but it will be much more difficult to do without topsoil.

5. POPULATION GROWTH—The overarching factor that makes all the other problems worse, especially when it is linked with pervasive poverty, is the uncontrolled global birth rate.

———————

—Special to *The Worst of Everything* from Norman Myers, Ph.D., environmental consultant and author of *The Primary Source*.

Thorough as he is, Dr. Myers has evidently overlooked recent American leaders, bacon, and New Year's Eve.

Not Fit for a Dog

The 9 Worst Enemies of Animal Life, According to Cleveland Amory

1. THE U.S. GOVERNMENT—Watt symbolized the attitude of Fish & Wildlife, the Department of Interior, the Navy. They shoot burros at China Lake and goats at San Clemente.

2. PENNSYLVANIA FISH & GAME DEPARTMENT—They shoot everything that moves.

3. MICHIGAN DEPARTMENT OF NATURAL RESOURCES—They're nuts with rifles. They OK bow hunting too.

4. WYOMING FISH & GAME DEPARTMENT—Starvation is their offical policy. They refuse to feed deer.

5. WOUND LABORATORIES (DEPARTMENT OF DEFENSE)—They shoot goats and pigs to simulate human wounds. They used to shoot dogs too.

6. WILD RANCH, TX—You pick off animals from your car as if you were picking them from a catalog.

7. CALIFORNIA FISH & GAME—They gave us Ray Arnett, director of the U.S. Fish & Wildlife Service, the man who said, "The only way to count mountain lions is to shoot them."

8. COLORADO FISH & GAME DEPARTMENT—They have a 1-shot antelope hunt. Watt goes on it. Too bad they don't shoot each other.

9. DETROIT ZOO—It is one of a wide variety of zoos I hate. I don't like to see animals imprisoned.

—Special to *The Worst of Everything* from Cleveland Amory, author, critic, and president of the Fund for Animals, Inc.

If I could have gotten into Imelda Marcos's closets (Lord knows there was room enough for me and all of Cleveland), I suspect we could have included her on the list. How many alligators died for her pumps?

Please Pick the Daisies Instead

The 12 Most Threatened Plants on Earth

African violet
Bamboo cycad
Drury slip orchid
Flor de mayo lenoso
Giant rafflesia
Kauai silversword
Neogomesia cactus
Phillip Island hibiscus
Palenque mahogany
Socotran pomegranate
Tarout cypress
Yeheb nut bush

—Selected by the International Union for Conservation of Nature and Natural Resources (IUCN).

One hesitates to mention these for fear, well justified, that some will show up on the bridal bouquet list for some Hollywood nuptial gala next week. Just pray, if you love nature, that you're the one who gets the card under your plate saying you can take the centerpiece home.

Beastly Fate

The 12 Most Threatened Animals on Earth

Bumblebee bat
Kouprey (Southeast Asian wild cattle)
Wooly spider monkey
Mediterranean monk seal
Pygmy hog
Northern white rhinoceros
Kagu (New Caledonian bird)
Sumatran rhinoceros
Angonoka (land tortoise)
Orinoco crocodile
Queen Alexandra's birdwing
Hawaiian or Oahu land snails

————

—Selected by the International Union for Conservation of Nature and Natural Resources (IUCN).

Wasn't that Pia Zadora I saw in a bumblebee-bat stole at the Oscars?

Paradises Lost, Soon

The 11 Most Threatened Nature Preserves on Earth

Arguaia National Park, Brazil
Juan Fernandez National Park, Chile
Krkonose National Park, Czechoslovakia
Kutai Game Reserve, Indonesia

Tai National Park, Ivory Coast
Manu National Park, Peru
Mount Apo National Park, the Philippines
Ngorongoro Conservation Area, Tanzania
John Pennekamp Coral Reef State Park and Key Largo National Marine Sanctuary, Florida
Durmitor National Park, Yugoslavia
Garmaba National Park, Zaire

—Selected by the International Union for Conservation of Nature and Natural Resources (IUCN).

New York's Central Park does not qualify, unless we amend the title to read, "Most Threats in a Nature Preserve."

Someone Is Missing a Link

The 3 Worst Hoaxes of Human History, According to Stephen J. Gould

1. PILTDOWN MAN—It commanded a good deal of attention, but it was a pretty poor fake. A skull purportedly unearthed by lawyer Charles Dawson in East Sussex, England, in 1908 and said to be that of the earliest ancestor of humans was, in fact, a modern human skull linked to an ape's jaw.

2. THE LYING STONES OF DR. BERINGER—Among the discoveries touted by the eighteenth-century German physician were two tablets containing the Ten Commandments. (A different historical context at that time permitted these bits of stone to be considered along with fossils.) But this "discovery" was, of course, a farce; it caused a great deal of controversy at the time.

3. THE CARDIFF GIANT—The supposed impression of a giant was discovered in upstate New York. The thing never

had any place in evolutionary history; a farmer sculpted it. But it is a curiosity, and can still be seen in Cooperstown, next to the Baseball Hall of Fame.

—Special to *The Worst of Everything* from Stephen J. Gould, professor of paleontology, biology, and history of science at Harvard University, columnist for *Natural History,* and an American Book Award winner.

All right, this isn't exactly a climatic or environmental issue. But like everything Gould has to say, I find it interesting and well beyond my familiarity. I would have said Bigfoot, Yeti, and Alley Oop.

I Thought I Saw a Theosaurus

The 5 Worst Dinosaur Myths, According to John Noble Wilford

1. DINOSAURS AND CAVE DWELLERS LIVED AT THE SAME TIME—Actually dinosaurs died out 65 million years ago, and the earliest hominids date back perhaps no more than 4 million years.

2. DINOSAURS DIED OUT IN THE ICE AGE—The last ice age, to which this myth presumably refers, ended 10,000 years ago.

3. ALL DINOSAURS WERE HUGE MONSTERS—Some were as small as crows and rabbits.

4. DINOSAURS BECAME EXTINCT BECAUSE THEY WERE DIM-WITTED, OVERGROWN, AND OBSOLETE—True, they had relatively small brains, but they did very well for 160 million years, an enviable record. Their extinction coincided with the demise of countless other species of animals and plants, suggesting some widespread environmental causes.

5. Dinosaurs Were Lethargic and Lived in Swamps
   —Some were and did. But many others were fleet and agile creatures that inhabited the dry plains, foraging over a
   great range and hunting in packs.

—Special to *The Worst of Everything* from John Noble Wilford, science correspondent for the *New York Times* and author of *The Riddle of the Dinosaur*.

*I'd add a sixth myth—that dinosaurs are still alive in Loch
Ness, the Congo, and the L. A. Raiders locker room. What is
around and just as big are whales, so let's concentrate on extin-
guishing them.*

BUSINESS
AND POLITICAL
WORSTS

Strange bedfellows indeed. Certainly they are turning up in the sack more often, and often, at least, metaphorically, together, en route to twin bunks in the Big House if we're lucky, the White House if we're not.

It is not surprising, all things considered, that we find ourselves politically just where we were 15 years ago—a miscreant attorney general, a bunch of law-skirting patriotic foot soldiers, and a President who claims he didn't have anything to do with carrying out a crooked policy that follows his beliefs to the tee. We haven't learned our Santayana, so we're bound to repeat history.

And politicians continue to be corrupted by what is, by business standards, chump change. What's new, however, is the truly big-bucks swindling of Ivan Boesky and other Wall Street insiders. With all the rules made their way, they still went outside them to reap outrageous profits. And businesspeople, judging by the popularity of business books and magazines and bank recruiters on campus, are our new gods. As for the more traditional God, his or her name has been taken in vain by a bunch of high-rolling, throat-cutting hustlers.

It's a neat trinity of corruption we've got going now, heaped on a false prosperity our children will be paying for decades after the record deficits have hit the fan. A compelling case could be made for our times as being the true Dickensian era—the best of times, the worst of times.

Here's a bit of tribute to the men and women who helped make it so. And let those of us who voted, canvased, contributed, and reported cast the first stone at the names herein. We could use lots of rocks and rock throwers.

•

WORSTS IN BUSINESS

Don't Call Us

Robert Half's Choices for the 10 Worst Résumés

1. EXPERIENCE—"Calculator, typewriter, documented forms, printout, and hickeys," from a secretarial candidate.

2. REASON FOR LEAVING LAST JOB—"Fired, fired, fired, fired, fired," from an accountant.

3. PERSONAL—"My mother lives with me. She is 69 years old and can travel."

4. SKILLS—"Excelent writen and verbal skils."

5. CURRENT EMPLOYMENT—"I have left my employer in Mexico and am presently home finishing treatment for my dysentery."

6. HEALTH—"Wear eyeglasses and have weakness in the toes."

7. PERSONAL—"Married 1969 Chevrolet."

8. RESTRICTIONS—"Will relocate anywhere except Russia, Red China, Vietnam or New York City."

9. PERSONAL—"Wife—immaculate. I am also a Notary Republic."

10. EXPERIENCE—"Prior experience in pubic accounting."

—Special to *The Worst of Everything* from Robert Half, president of Robert Half International, Inc., one of the world's largest personnel firms.

Don't Go Anywhere with It

The 4 Most Common Credit Card Misbillings

	% of Misbillings
1. Charged twice or charged for item not purchased	45.2
2. Payment not credited or credited incorrectly	21.8
3. Charged for another's purchases	17.6
4. Refund not credited	7.3

—From Jeffrey Feinman, *The Money Lists*, Doubleday, Dolphin, New York, 1981.

For #5 I'd add a Honda mechanic of my acquaintance who had $50,000 in phone bills mysteriously tacked onto his month's tab. He evidently lost his credit card to a gang of gabby international thieves or to an astronaut calling his mother from the Van Allen belt.

Buy Now, Pay Later

The 3 Worst Months in Which to Buy Stock*

	Average Loss, %
1. September	−1.2
2. May	−0.9
3. February	−0.3

*Based on figures from 1928–1983. All other months recorded net gains, with July (2.0%) showing the highest.

—From *Standard & Poor's Corporation*, September 27, 1984.

Money Talks

The 4 Worst Threats to American Business
Prosperity, According to Malcolm Forbes

1. PROTECTIONISM—Severe restrictions on trade caused the great depression. They can do so again. Protectionism rarely, if ever, helps the intended beneficiary and ends up hurting the rest of us.

2. THE FEDERAL RESERVE—Volcker, Greenspan and their colleagues believe that prosperity causes inflation. They don't think that we can grow faster than 3 percent without a resurgence of rising prices. They slowed the economy in 1984–1985, unnecessarily. They can do so again in the future.

3. BUDGET DEFICIT—In and of itself, the budget deficit will not ruin America. The greater danger right now is what Congress might do in the name of fighting this big shortfall—raise taxes significantly. That would be truly harmful.

4. ECONOMISTS—Too often this profession loses sight of a basic truth when it comes to evaluating economic policy—the importance of incentive. If a policy encourages people to be successful, to be more productive, to be more innovative, then it is to be applauded. Economics need to spend less time on mathematics and more time on observing the real world.

—Special to *The Worst of Everything* from Malcolm S. Forbes, Jr., president and chief operating officer of *Forbes* magazine.

Note that, unlike Gephardt and many other trade-unbalanced Americans, Mr. Forbes doesn't blame the Japanese for being more industrious, honest, and imaginative than we are.

It Seemed Like a Good Way to Kill

*The 10 Most Expensive U.S. Military Project Cancellations**

	Cost, $ Million
1. B-IA bomber (1968–1977)	4758.7
2. Sgt. York DIVAD (1977–1985)	1800.0
3. Manned orbiting laboratory (1964–1970)	1491.0
4. XB-70 bomber (1958–1967)	1468.0
5. Roland SA missile (1975–1984)	1300.0
6. Navaho cruise missile (1954–1957)	679.8
7. Snark cruise missile (1947–1962)	677.4
8. ANP nuclear airplane (1951–1961)	511.6
9. Rascal AS missile (1946–1958)	448.0
10. Skybolt AS missile (1960–1963)	440.0

*For the years 1946–1985.

—From the Center for Defense Information.

This is, believe it or not, the good news. Imagine if we had built these things.

Take Your Business Elsewhere (Part I)

*The 10 Worst States for Business Climate**

1. Michigan

2. Oregon

3. Ohio

4. Rhode Island

5. Illinois

6. Minnesota

7. Wisconsin

8. Pennsylvania

9. West Virginia

10. New York

*Criteria used are labor costs, productivity, unionization, energy costs, local taxes, debts, welfare expenditures, and environmental regulations.

—From *General Manufacturing Business Climates*, Alexander Grant & Company, Minneapolis, MN, 1984.

We wanted Robert Vesco's rating on this matter, but the post office can't provide us with a forwarding address.

Take Your Business Elsewhere (Part II)

The 10 Worst States for Small Business, According to Inc. *Magazine**

1. Wyoming

2. North Dakota

3. Montana

4. Oklahoma

5. Iowa

6. South Dakota

7. Louisiana

8. Nebraska

9. Idaho

10. West Virginia

*Composite rating based upon capital resources, labor, taxes, and other factors influencing the climate for small businesses.

—From *Inc. Magazine*, October 1987.

In Bad Company

The 10 Least Admired Companies in America, According to Fortune*

1. Financial Corporation of America
2. LTV
3. Pan Am
4. American Motors
5. Mansville
6. Control Data
7. Amex
8. BankAmerica
9. Crown Zellerbach
10. Bethlehem Steel

*From a poll of 8000 executives, outside directors, and financial analysts, who were asked to rate the 10 largest companies in their own industry (or the industry they follow) on 8 key attributes: quality of management; quality of products or services; innovativeness; long-term investment value; financial soundness; ability to attract, develop, and keep talented people; community and environmental responsibility; and use of corporate assets.

—From *Fortune*, January 6, 1986.

We're talking pre–O-ring failure on the space shuttle or we might add Morton Thiokol. And pre-Irangate, which lets out all Richard Secord's hundreds of patriotic corporate creations.

Into the Valley of Death Rode the 500

The 5 Fortune 500 Companies with the Worst
Return to Investors over 10 Years (1974–1984)

	Return, %
1. Tosco	−6.99
2. Mansville	−6.57
3. Inspiration Resources	−5.46
4. International Harvester	−4.46
5. Phelps Dodge	−3.83

—From *Fortune*, April 29, 1985.

All I want to know is how my broker convinced me to buy into each of these.

Keeping Bad Company

The 10 Corporations with the Worst Reputations

1. Exxon

2. Mobil

3. Gulf

4. AT&T

5. Citicorp

6. Con Edison

7. Xerox

8. Equitable Life

9. IBM

10. Various bank charge cards

—From Jeffrey Feinman, *The Money Lists*, Doubleday, Dolphin, New York, 1981.

This ranking seems, understandably, to have much to do with the frequency with which we pay gasoline, telephone, electricity, insurance, and credit card bills. I'm surprised therefore that Gannett Knight-Ridder and other newspaper chains aren't at the top, since we plunk down our quarters every day for those birdcage liners and fish wrappers.

Is This My Paycheck or My Cab Fare?

The 10 Worst Employers for Hourly Wages

1. Hotels

2. Clothing stores

3. Laundries

4. Leather-goods manufacturers

5. Clothing manufacturers

6. General merchandise stores

7. Textile mills

8. Furniture manufacturers

9. Furniture and appliance stores

10. Food stores

—From Jeffrey Feinman, *The Money Lists*, Doubleday, Dolphin, New York, 1981.

There are many, however, well known to the bellhops, who earn a good hourly wage in hotels, even if not employed by those establishments. No doubt the owners of many of the businesses on this list give daily thanks to the easy movement of illegal aliens. If you can't get an American for slave wages, you can always take advantage of those who don't know the language, or the rules.

The Worst Place to Leave the Lights On

The 10 Utilities Sending Out
the Highest Average Annual Bills

		Ave Ann Bill, $
1.	Consolidated Edison, NY	1318
2.	San Diego Gas and Electric	1117
3.	Long Island Lighting, NY	984
4.	Hawaiian Electric	953
5.	United Illuminating, CT	882
6.	Public Service Electric & Gas, NJ	877
7.	Northern Indiana Public Service	856
8.	Connecticut Light and Power	838
9.	Boston Edison, MA	814
10.	Narragansett Electric, RI	753

—From Richard Boyer and David Savageau, *Places Rated Almanac*, Rand McNally, Chicago, 1985 (U.S. Dept. of Energy, 1983).

For those who wondered how Con Ed got on the most-hated corporations list, look no further. Why does it cost 50 percent more to run your toaster in New York than in any other of the most expensive places to do so? I can't think of a good reason. Con Ed doesn't have to. Unless you've got your own windmill, babbling brook, or hunk of plutonium, you haven't got much choice. I might have mentioned southern exposure, but New York doesn't get enough sunlight to consider that source.

Lifeboats for the Rich and Famous

The 10 States with the Fewest Millionaires

		Millionaires/100,000 Population
1.	Wyoming	29
2.	Nevada	35

3. Arkansas	44
4. Utah	56
5. West Virginia	65
6. Maryland, DC	86
7. New Hampshire	97
8. Oregon	102
9. Arizona	115
10. Missouri	123

—From National Wealth Survey, U.S. Trust of New York, 1980.

Nevada has, however, the lead in another related category—changing the status of the most millionaires. It's not the gambling as much as the alimony. If it weren't for Wayne Newton, Paul Anka, and assorted mafiosi, think where the state would rank on this list.

It Could Be Worse. It Was.

The 10 Worst Years for American Unemployment

	Unemployment Rate, %
1. 1933	24.9
2. 1932	23.6
3. 1934	21.7
4. 1935	20.1
5. 1938	19.0
6. 1939	17.2
7. 1936	17.0
8. 1931	15.9
9. 1940	14.5
10. 1937	14.3

—From Jeffrey Feinman, *The Money Lists*, Doubleday, Dolphin, New York, 1981.

Bless My W-2

The 10 Worst Countries for Taxation*

		Ave Ann per Capita Tax, $
1.	Sweden	6933
2.	Norway	6771
3.	Denmark	5068
4.	France	4532
5.	Netherlands	4484
6.	Switzerland	4475
7.	Belgium	4386
8.	Canada	4181
9.	German Federated Republic	4133
10.	United States	3832

*For those who want to know, the best country is Portugal, with an annual per capita rate of $746.

—From an International Monetary Fund survey, 1981.

The sex and drugs may be cheap or even free in the top 3 countries, but there is, evidently, a tab. At least for our money we get weapons that don't work. All they get is hospitalization, housing, and a decent wage. And sex and drugs.

Take This Job and Shove It

The 9 Worst Countries for Job Hours*

		Hr/Wk
1.	Malaysia (Sabah)	53.0
2.	Republic of Korea	52.5
3.	Sri Lanka	50.4
4.	Peru	49.6
5.	Costa Rica	49.3

6. Singapore	49.1
7. Brunei	48.8
8. Iceland	48.7
9. Hong Kong	47.8

*Nonagricultural.

—From *Yearbook of Labour Statistics*, International Labor Organization, 1984.

The worst part about #3 is that you're liable, after a long week's work, to get blown up on the bus ride home. In Brunei they work harder to support the American President in his bid to support Nicaraguan rebels without the support of his own populace or government.

Go Tell It on the Union

The 10 Worst Major Cities on Earth for Weekly Wages

	$/Wk*
1. Tientsin	8.76
2. Beijing	9.08
3. Shanghai	9.46
4. Jakarta	34.00
5. Bombay	35.00
6. Manila	43.00
7. Cairo	49.00
8. Bangkok	64.00
9. Istanbul	82.00
10. Mexico City	87.00

*Rated between 1979 and 1983.

—From John T. Marlin, Immanuel Ness, and Stephen T. Collins, *Book of World City Rankings*, Free Press, New York, 1986.

All right, it looks bad. But perhaps the meal money, transportation allowance, and "golden parachute" retirement programs are outstanding in Tientsin.

Only Maynard G. Krebs Could Love It

The 10 Worst Major Cities on Earth for Employment

	% Unemployed*
1. Liverpool	20.4
2. Glasgow	19.7
3. Naples	19.0
4. Detroit	17.7
5. Manchester	17.3
6. Birmingham	16.1
7. Amsterdam	15.0
8. Dublin	14.6
9. Marseilles	14.2
10. Leeds	13.1

*Rated between 1980 and 1982.

—From Richard Boyer and David Savageau, *Places Rated Almanac*, Rand McNally, C'iicago, 1985.

The totals for #1 do not include Ringo Starr, who, as far as I can tell, hasn't done anything but wine commercials in a decade.

WORSTS IN POLITICS

Don't Vote for Me

The 4 Worst Campaign Gaffes, According to
William Schneider

1. The Republicans called the Democratic Party the party of "Rum, Romanism and Rebellion" at a campaign dinner at Delmonico's Hotel in 1884. The statement helped elect the first Democratic president since the Civil War, Grover Cleveland. ·

2. Gerald Ford in 1976 said that Poland was not under Soviet domination. The country said, "Jesus Christ, he's the President; did he really say that?"

3. Gary Hart indulged in monkey business and destroyed his candidacy in 1987.

4. In 1972 George McGovern pledged "1000 percent" support for vice-presidential candidate Tom Eagleton when the Missouri senator was found to have formerly been under psychiatric treatment, then subsequently withdrew his support.

—Special to *The Worst of Everything* from William Schneider of the American Enterprise Institute in Washington, DC, called "the nation's hot new political pundit" by *Newsweek*.

Pay attention now, we've switched to politics. From business to monkey business. Which brings us to #3. Was it really a mistake? Is it really over? Would he rather have had Donna Rice or the whole country?

Yawn to the Chief

The 3 Worst Presidential Speakers, According to
William Schneider

1. JIMMY CARTER—No emotion. And remember when we
   called Humphrey "Hubert Horatio Hornblower"? Carter's
   accent—"Eye-talian votes"—didn't help.

2. LYNDON BAINES JOHNSON—"Ma Fella Americans, I come
   to you with a heavy heart. . . ." Can't you hear it still?

3. RICHARD NIXON—"I am not a crook." But he was a
   bore.

Not that it matters. They all got elected anyway, which shows
just how important speaking ability is.

———————

—Special to *The Worst of Everything* from William Schneider of the American Enterprise Institute in Washington, DC, called "the nation's hot new
political pundit" by *Newsweek*.

*Mr. Schneider might have included Gerald Ford had Ford
ever given a speech, or for that matter, given anything except a
pardon and a few pratfalls.*

The Address for Which State of the Union?

The 9 Worst-Schooled Presidents*

George Washington
Andrew Jackson
Martin Van Buren
Zachary Taylor
Millard Fillmore
Abraham Lincoln
Andrew Johnson

Grover Cleveland
Harry Truman

*Never attended college

———

—From Joseph Nathan Kane, *Facts about the Presidents*, Wilson, New York, 1968.

And then there are those—they would make a far longer list— for whom the schooling didn't take.

Say It Ain't So, Ronnie

Ronald Reagan's Biggest Lie (and Some Others), According to James Barber

Ronald's Reagan's biggest lie is projecting the image that he is a realist; this has the biggest negative impact on political discourse. He lives in Oz and his criterion of validity is theatrical, not empirical. This allows him to claim such things as:

He starred in a play about a dying World War I lieutenant while he was at Eureka College. He wasn't even in the play.

Racial integration began in World War II when a black cook shot down a Japanese Zero at Pearl Harbor. Reagan told the story many times in the 1980 campaign. The incident never happened, and besides, the armed forces were already integrated. Yet Reagan says "I remember it well; it was a very powerful scene."

He was in Europe during the war, photographing the liberation of concentration camps; he was, in fact, in Hollywood making movies.

There is more oil in Alaska than in Saudi Arabia.

Trees cause dangerous air pollution.

Missiles launched from submarines are recallable.

The Reykjavik summit was the dawn of new hope in U.S.-Soviet arms negotiations; the summit actually collapsed in failure.

There is as much forest in the U.S. now as there was when Washington was at Valley Forge.

The U.S. is not trying to overthrow the Nicaraguan government.

People who sleep on grates "are homeless, you might say, by choice."

The South African government has "eliminated segregation that we once had in our country—the type of thing where hotels and restaurants and places of entertainment and so forth were segregated—that has all been eliminated."

"Nuclear power is the cleanest, the most efficient, and the most economical energy source, with no environmental problems."

"The only thing I know about major shipments of arms [to Iran] is... everything that we sold them could be put in one cargo plane, and there would be plenty of room left over."

"We did not, repeat, did not trade weapons or anything else for hostages—nor will we."

—Special to *The Worst of Everything* from James David Barber, professor of political science at Duke University and author of *The Presidential Character*. Several "misstatements" are taken from a *People* magazine compilation.

The Pot Calling the Kettle

Richard Nixon's 20 Worst Enemies

Alexander E. Barkan, AFL-CIO Committee on Political Education
John Conyers, Michigan congressman
Maxwell Dane, Doyle, Dane Bernbach, advertising agency

Sid Davidoff, aide to Mayor John Lindsay of New York
Ronald Dellums, California congressman
S. Harrison Dogole, Globe Security System
Charles Dyson, Dyson-Kissner Corporation
Bernard T. Field, Council for a Livable World
Ed Guthman, *Los Angeles Times*
Morton Halprin, Common Cause
Samuel M. Lambert, National Educational Association
Allard Lowenstein, New York congressman
Mary McGrory, Washington newspaper columnist
Stewart Rawlings Mott, General Motors heir and philanthropist
S. Sterling Munro, Jr., congressional aide
Paul Newman, movie actor
Arnold M. Picker, United Artists Corporation
Daniel Schorr, CBS News correspondent
Howard Stein, Dreyfus Corporation
Leonard Woodcock, United Auto Workers

—As presented by John Dean to the Senate Watergate committee on June 27, 1973.

Were I so inclined, which I am, I might wish to improve this list by including Nixon himself, truth, and fair play high on the list.

Software Is for Soft Minds

The 5 Worst Congressional Enemies of High Tech*

Rep. John LaFalce (D, NY)
Rep. Daniel Rostenkowski (D, IL)
Rep. Fortney Start (D, CA)
Sen. Lowell Weicker (R, CT)
Rep. Stanley Ludine (D, NY)

*Criteria used were voting record, political clout, and proximity to fertile high-tech fields.

—Selected by *Electronic Business*, 1985.

This Weicker guy manages to be both another enemy of Nixon and an enemy of high tech. Perhaps it was Rosemary Woods's state-of-the-art tape recorder that turned the senator away from technology.

Franking, I Don't Give a Damn

The 10 Senators Who Spent the Most Taxpayer Money Sending Out Mass Mailings

	$/Resident, 3 Mos*
1. Dodd (D, CT)	.19
2. Grassley (R, IA)	.17
3. Pressler (R, SD)	.16
4. Andrews (R, ND)	.12
4. Abdnor (R, SD)	.12
6. Denton (R, AL)	.11
7. Simpson (R, WY)	.08
7. Murkowski (R, AK)	.08
7. Hatch (R, UT)	.08
7. Roth (R, DE)	.08

*July–September 1985.

—From the Secretary of the Senate.

Do you know how you can get the post office to take you off the list for junk mail? Does that apply here? I can see how Hatch needs to send a lot of mail. It's not easy convincing people that Ollie North is a hero.

Who Elected These Guys (Part I)

*The 18 Worst-Voting Senators, According to Liberals**

Murkowski (R, AK)
Armstrong (R, CO)

Mattingly (R, GA)
McClure (R, ID)
Symms (R, ID)
Quayle (R, IN)
Dole (R, KS)
Hecht (R, NV)
Laxalt (R, NV)
East (R, NC)
Helms (R, NC)
Nickles (R, OK)
Thurmond (R, SC)
Abdnor (R, SD)
Gramm (R, TX)
Garn (R, UT)
Trible (R, VA)
Wallop (R, WY)

*As rated by Americans for Democratic Action, according to voting records, 1985, on a gamut of judicial, social, economic, foreign, and military policy issues.

Who Elected These Guys (Part II)

The 16 Worst-Voting Senators, According to Conservatives*

Hart (D, CO)
Sarbanes (D, MD)
Cranston (D, CA)
Kennedy (D, MA)
Riegle (D, MI)
Dodd (D, CT)
Lautenberg (D, NJ)
Levin (D, MI)
Matsunaga (D, HI)
Metzenbaum (D, OH)
Mitchell (D, ME)
Pell (D, RI)
Inouye (D, HI)

Tsongas (D, MA)
Sasser (D, TN)
Leahy (D, VT)

*As rated by Free Congress PAC 1984, according to voting records on 234 votes, on a gamut of judicial, social, economic, foreign, and military policy issues.

Who Elected These Guys (Part III)

The 16 Worst-Voting Representatives, According to Liberals*

Callahan (R, AL)
Stump (R, AZ)
Rudd (R, AZ)
Kolbe (R, AZ)
Badham (R, CA)
Craig (R, ID)
Hillis (R, IN)
Livingston (R, LA)
Lott (R, MS)
Skeen (R, NM)
Cobey (R, NC)
Miller (R, OH)
Spence (R, SC)
Boulter (R, TX)
Slaughter (R, VA)
Cheney (R, WY)

*As rated by the Americans for Democratic Action, according to voting records, 1985, on a gamut of judicial, social, economic, foreign, and military policy issues.

Who Elected These Guys (Part IV)

*The 14 Worst-Voting Representatives, According to Conservatives**

Berman (D, CA)
Lehman, William (D, FL)
Clay (D, MO)
Garcia (D, NY)
Edwards (D, CA)
Hawkins (D, CA)
Roybal (D, CA)
Addabbo (D, NY)
Burton (D, CA)
Gray (D, PA)
Matsui (D, CA)
Mitchell (D, MD)
Torres (D, CA)
Waxman (D, CA)

*As rated by Free Congress PAC, according to voting records on 363 votes, 1984, on a gamut of judicial, social, economic, foreign and military policy issues.

You Vote for Me, I Won't Vote (Part I)

The 13 Senators with the Worst Voting Records

	% Bills Voted on, 1984–1985
1. East (R, NC)*	46
2. Stennis (D, MS)	73
3. Goldwater (R, AZ)*	77
4. Mathias (R, MD)	83
4. Chiles (D, FL)*	83
6. Hatfield (R, OR)	85
7. Laxalt (R, NV)	86
8. Inouye (D, HI)	87

9. Armstrong (R, CO)	88
10. Stevens (R, AK)	90
10. Garn (R, UT)	90
10. Murkowski (R, AK)	90
10. Exon (D, NE)	90

*Missed 1 day or more because of illness or death in the family.

—From the *Congressional Quarterly,* 1986.

You Vote for Me, I Won't Vote (Part II)

The 10 Representatives with the Worst Voting Records

	% Bills Voted on, 1984–1985
1. Addabbo (D, NY)*	58
2. Hefner (D, NC)*	73
3. Nelson (D, FL)	73
4. Wilson (D, TX)	74
5. Heftel (D, HI)	75
6. Conyers (D, MI)	75
7. Dymally (D, FL)	76
8. Loeffler (R, TX)	76
9. O'Brien (R, IL)	77
10. McKinney (R, CT)*	77

*Missed 1 day or more because of illness or death in the family.

—From the *Congressional Quarterly,* 1986.

These are the easy targets. What we need are statistics on most sessions slept through, most junkets taken, most pointless filibusters, pork-barrel deals, pressure-group cave-ins. We don't have those figures, but I'll wager someone in the White House does. But I wouldn't want to wake him.

Coneheads of State

The 5 Worst Presidential Candidates for 1988

Here we offer a list of our own churlish derivation. When it comes to naming the worst, you have to include an assessment of sideshow, the presidential hat toss. Only those with the following qualifications need apply to participate in that carnival: male; between 35 and death; white (c'mon, Jesse, get serious); non-Jewish (don't bother, Ed); willing to smile, equivocate, cut deals, forfeit privacy and family life, and keep within a political spectrum as narrow as Catherine Deneuve's acting range. If you seen one you seen 'em all, but here's the worst of the worst of today's chapeau careeners:

1. GEORGE BUSH—He gives fresh meaning to the word "milquetoast." Underneath his elitist snobbery and mindless waffling is the heart of Ronald Reagan and the backbone of an invertebrate. If he weren't Reagan's man, he'd be no man at all.

2. MICHAEL DUKAKIS—His idea of a smile is a wince, and he hasn't laughed since the Red Sox last won a World Series. He had the good fortune to be running against a moron (Edward King) for governor, in a state with enough smart types to make its economy hum and its governor look good. Even then he only beat the moron the second time around.

3. ALEXANDER HAIG—No one but him takes his candidacy seriously, but then he's already played President once before, seizing the microphones from the ordinarily braindead Ronald Reagan. He's master of the malaprop, and a hothead to boot. The only chance we'd have to avoid nuclear war under Haig is if his button-pressing finger got jammed in his fruit salad.

4. RICHARD GEPHARDT—Someone tried to stuff Jimmy Carter's teeth into Robert Redford's head, and Gephardt is the unhappy result. The only idea competing with the teeth

for space is a Neanderthal notion of penalizing foreigners for making things better than we do, thereby encouraging American manufacturers to keep screwing up.

5. ROBERT DOLE—He's no relation to the pineapple but just as canned. He worked his way up the legislative ladder carrying an applause sign for Republican presidents, but now he bites the hand that fed him. His wife is just as power-hungry, so at least we have a happy DC couple. Dole looks like Dick Nixon. If, like the Fugitive, you seek a one-armed man, write in Inouye.

DEATH AND DESTRUCTION WORSTS

If you are the cautious type, be forewarned: Tulsa, OK, is a bad place to take a ride, not to mention the whole state of Wyoming and most of central Europe. Driving a car is not good for you, but driving a hydroplane is the worst idea, short of signing up for the next shuttle.

Jog, if you live in West Virginia. And wherever you live, watch out for aspirin overdosing—it's the #15 cause of drug deaths. Keep Grandpa away from the stairs and don't go into labor in Addis Ababa.

If you heed all the statistics, you may well never leave your house. But to stay home isn't safe either. So go, and go forewarned. Wherever you go, you'll find new and interesting ways to wake up dead. You'll find more of them in New York City than anywhere else in this country. But dead may be the best way to see the Big Apple after all.

If you live long enough to finish the upcoming chapter, you can take some comfort in knowing that no matter how much snow has piled up in your driveway, 20,000 folk in Yungay, Peru, never got near their shovels in history's worst avalanche. And the Spanish flu gave 50 million people an Excedrin headache that wouldn't quit, so don't complain about your migraines.

Just lie down, read this chapter, and, if you start to get queasy, take 2 aspirin (no more). You also might consider strapping on a helmet, particularly if you live in Massachusetts. You never know when you might fall out of bed.

Shake, Rattle, and Kill

The 10 Worst Snakes to Be Bitten By

1. KING COBRA—At 18 feet, this native of the Burmese jungles is the largest of all venomous snakes. Its bite, packed with large quantities of venom, causes a high mortality rate among victims.

2. TAIPAN—This Australian 10-footer is shy and quick. It bites savagely, injecting a highly potent neurotoxin which can cause death within 24 hours.

3. **Mamba**—This 14-foot black or green African snake is unusually agile and aggressive, and may be the only deliberate stalker of humans among the venomous snakes.

4. **Bushmaster**—Largest of the pit vipers, the bushmaster occupies abandoned animal burrows in Central America. It has fangs over an inch in length through which it injects massive doses of toxin when provoked. Left alone, it is generally sluggish and unaggressive.

5. **Western Diamondback Rattler**—Most dangerous of the American rattlesnakes, the western diamondback kills 10 to 20 people a year. Its venom causes severe local tissue damage, frequently necessitating amputation.

6. **Fer-de-Lance**—Found only on Martinique, this active snake has a bite that injects large quantities of venom, which spreads throughout the body and causes internal bleeding.

7. **Tropical Rattlesnake**—This active Central and South American rattler has a venom 10 times more potent than the western rattler's.

8. **Tiger Snake**—A high percentage of Australian snakebite deaths are attributed to this 6-foot snake. The bite induces pain, vomiting, dulling drunkenness, sweating, and circulatory collapse.

9. **Common Cobra**—The fabled cobra used by Indian snake charmers has enough venom in 1 bite to kill 30 people. Commonly found around human habitations, but it is generally a shy hunter of frogs and rats.

10. **Jarracussu**—This aquatic South American snake has a deadly bite, though it causes "only" blindness and extensive tissue damage more often than it causes death.

—From *Dangerous to Man* by Roger Caras, for which book Dr. Sherman Minton of the Department of Microbiology, Indiana University, a leading authority on venomous animals, selected the 10 snakes he'd "least like to be locked up in a phone booth with."

Reminds me of that joke about the 2 men in the desert. One gets bitten in a private place by a rattler. He sends the other for help. Friend finds a doctor, tells him about the bite but not where. Doctor says "Make an incision and suck out the poison." Friend runs back, finds victim writhing in agony. "What did Doc say?" mumbles the bitee. "Doc says you're goin' to die." If the snakes don't get you, the jokes will.

No Retirement Plan

The 9 Worst Jobs for Staying Alive In

	Deaths/1000 Workers
1. Astronaut	30.0
2. Hydroplane driver	25.0
2. Race-car driver	25.0
4. Aerial performer (without net)	8.0
4. Boxer	8.0
6. Lumberworker	6.2
7. Skin diver or helmet diver	4.0
8. Power-line worker	3.4
9. Steeple climber	2.8

—From the Society of Actuaries.

These estimates were compiled before the shuttle disaster. How much of the new NASA budget goes to flight insurance now I don't know, but the crash suggests yet another reason to choose a different final frontier for expensive grandstanding.

Passport to Oblivion

The 10 Countries with the Most Fatal Accidents

	Deaths/100,000 Population
1. Hungary	68.8
2. Austria	67.6
3. Venezuela	61.6
4. Luxembourg	61.1
5. Northern Ireland	56.2
6. Poland	54.7
7. West Germany	48.9
8. United States	48.4
8. Switzerland	48.4
9. Canada	48.0

—Data from countries reporting to the World Health Organization, 1977–1979.

This means—I should know better than to say it—that you stand a good chance of becoming goulash if you make a Pest of yourself. I've already thought twice about making Northern Ireland my home away from home, but Switzerland? Chocolate overdose? Standing too close to a cuckoo clock or a wayward fondue fork? Dropping Ollie's safe-deposit box on your foot? Other than that, I'm stumped. Certainly there are no train accidents.

An Accident's Waiting to Happen Here (Part I)

The 10 Worst U.S. Cities for Accidental Deaths

	Deaths/100,000 Population*
1. Tulsa, OK	88.6
2. Oklahoma City, OK	67.5
3. New Orleans, LA	65.3
4. Birmingham, AL	62.3

5. Kansas City, MO	62.0
6. Cleveland, OH	51.0
7. Phoenix, AZ	50.1
8. Dallas, TX	47.9
9. St. Louis, MO	47.2
10. Tucson, AZ	46.9

*National average=46.2

—From M. Hirsh Goldberg, *The Blunder Book*, Morrow, New York, 1984.

What is it about Oklahoma that is decidedly not OK? Are oil rigs so dangerous? Are the after-Sooner-game parties so wild?

An Accident's Waiting to Happen Here (Part II)

The 10 Worst States for Accidental Deaths

	*Deaths/100,000 Population**
1. Wyoming	85.8
2. Nevada	85.6
3. Montana	75.2
4. New Mexico	72.2
5. Mississippi	71.4
6. Idaho	63.9
7. Arizona	62.2
8. Louisiana	61.1
9. South Dakota	57.8
10. Alabama	57.7

*National average=46.2.

—From M. Hirsh Goldberg, *The Blunder Book*, Morrow, New York, 1984.

I'm not quite sure how accidents happen in these states. In the first several it would seem difficult to find anyone, let alone someone willing to inadvertently do you in. So what are the in-human ends? Colliding with a sheep, being mauled by a grizzly, or touching electrified cattle fencing? The only way to find out is to go there. But part of growing up is realizing that not all questions can or should be answered.

It Wasn't Supposed to End This Way

*The 8 Leading Causes of Accidental Death in the U.S.**

		Deaths
1.	Motor vehicles	52,600
2.	Falls	12,000
3.	Drowning	7,000
4.	Fires, burns, etc.	5,500
5.	Suffocation/choking	3,100
6.	Poison (liquid/solid)	2,800
7.	Firearms	1,800
8.	Poison (gas/vapor)	1,500

*Of 105,000 reported in 1980. Note: All other causes—falling objects, air travel, medical complications—accounted for 18,400 deaths.

—From M. Hirsh Goldberg, *The Blunder Book*, Morrow, New York, 1984.

I find #2 surprising. I know about William Holden and Billy Joe McAllister. But who else have you ever heard of who's died in a fall? Do they do it in the comfort of their own homes or off the Golden Gate Bridge? I know this sounds morbid, but inquiring minds want to know.

Get a Ranch House and Stay in It

The 20 Leading Causes of Accidental (Nonautomotive) Injuries

		Injuries*
1.	Stairs	763,000
2.	Bicycles and accessories	518,000
3.	Baseball	478,000
4.	Football	470,000
5.	Basketball	434,000
6.	Nails, carpet tacks, screws	244,000
7.	Chairs, sofas, sofa beds	236,000
8.	Skating	225,000
8.	Nonglass tables	225,000
10.	Glass doors, windows, panels	208,000
11.	Beds	199,000
12.	Playground equipment	165,000
13.	Lumber	151,000
14.	Cutlery and knives	140,000
14.	Glass bottles and jars	140,000
16.	Desks, cabinets, bookcases	126,000
16.	Swimming	126,000
18.	Drinking glasses	111,000
19.	Ladders and stools	99,000
19.	Fences	99,000

*Reported at hospital emergency rooms, July 1, 1980, through June 30, 1981.

—From the National Electronic Injury Surveillance System, Consumer Product Safety Commission.

Who am I to argue with the facts? Still I can't help wondering. Where are fork-in-toaster traumas, tongues caught in soda bottles, eyeballs lost to snapping towels, blindness induced by masturbation? Was my mother wrong all those years? I can't believe it.

Wear a Helmet to Bed

The 9 States with the Worst Rates for Death by Falling

	Deaths/100,000 Population
1. Massachusetts	13.1
2. Nebraska	11.9
3. Montana	11.2
4. Missouri	11.1
5. Ohio	10.9
6. Maine	10.7
7. Kentucky	10.5
8. Rhode Island	10.0
8. Kansas	10.0

—From the Statistical Bureau of the Metropolitan Life Insurance Company, 1970.

It is windy in Boston, but is someone purposely strewing banana peels on the streets? Those of us who live in houses should stay away from the basement steps. I'm moving my office upstairs.

The Case for Asbestos Underwear

The 10 States with the Worst Rates for Death by Accidental Immolation

	Deaths/100,000 Population
1. Alaska	10.3
2. Mississippi	7.2
3. South Carolina	6.6
4. New Mexico	5.8
4. Alabama	5.8

6. Georgia	5.6
7. North Carolina	4.8
8. Oklahoma	4.7
8. Louisiana	4.7
8. Tennessee	4.7

—From the Statistical Bureau of the Metropolitan Life Insurance Company, 1970.

Yes, if your sick mind works the same way mine does, we are talking baked Alaskans here. You should be ashamed of yourself, as am I.

Wear Water Wings in the Tub

The 12 States with the Worst Rates for Death by Accidental Drowning

	Deaths/100,000 Population
1. Alaska	8.6
2. Florida	6.8
3. Nevada	5.9
4. Louisiana	5.7
5. South Carolina	5.2
6. Mississippi	5.1
7. Idaho	5.0
8. Arkansas	4.8
8. Arizona	4.8
10. Delaware	4.5
10. Montana	4.5
10. New Mexico	4.5

—From the Statistical Bureau of the Metropolitan Life Insurance Company, 1970.

Is there a connection here to the preceding list? Do some die trying to douse the flames in Fairbanks? The sight of a gator may be sufficient to intimidate some swimmers in Sarasota, but Tahoe aside, I wasn't even aware there was any water in Nevada.

Pitter-Patter Went Your Heart

The 5 States with the Worst Rate for Death by Heart Disease

	Deaths/100,000 Population*
1. West Virginia	581.0
2. Kentucky	561.6
3. South Carolina	559.4
4. Louisiana	537.3
5. Pennsylvania	533.3

*Based on the age-adjusted death rate of white males, aged 35 to 74, 1980. The national average is 480.9.

—From the National Center for Health Statistics.

Take 200 Aspirin and Call the Morgue

*The 20 Worst Drug Killers in America**

1. Alcohol in combination with other drugs

2. Heroin/morphine

3. Codeine

4. Elavil

5. Valium

6. Darvon

7. Phenobarbital

8. Cocaine

9. PCP combinations

10. Methadone

11. Seconal

12. Tylenol, Datril

13. Sinequan

14. Placidyl

15. Aspirin

16. Nembutal

17. Doriden

18. Amytol

19. Dalmane

20. Methaqualone

*Based on 1982 medical examiner reports of deaths caused by drugs taken alone and in combination.

———

—From the Drug Abuse Warning Network, National Institute on Drug Abuse. The most common brand names are used here rather than generic names.

And I thought Bud McFarlane was a jerk for trying to OD on Valium. I figured if that's what he planned to take if the Ayatollah got him, the worst that could happen was that he'd confess under the dreamy conviction he was in a hot tub with Ollie. I figured wrong. I know next time I get a headache I'll consider toughing it out.

Ever Hear the One about the Polish Driver?

The 16 Worst Countries for Auto Deaths

		Deaths/100,000 Registered Vehicles
1.	Poland	164
2.	Greece	160
3.	Hungary	134
4.	Czechoslovakia	117
5.	Austria	104
6.	Ireland	97
7.	Spain	83
8.	West Germany	71
9.	Belgium	68
10.	Finland	66
11.	France	61
12.	Denmark	53
13.	Italy	50
14.	Switzerland	46
15.	Norway	44
15.	East Germany	44

—From the National Highway Safety Administration, 1975 statistics.

Supply your own joke, you sick bigot. I suspect this list is woefully incomplete, having driven—and barely lived to report it—in Central America, where touring is a blood sport.

For Whom the Toll Tolls

The 10 Most Dangerous State Highways

		Deaths/100 Million Vehicle Mi
1.	New York State Thruway	46
2.	New Jersey Turnpike	40

3. Florida Turnpike	36
4. Garden State Parkway	28
4. Oklahoma Turnpike	28
6. Ohio Turnpike	26
6. Illinois Tollway	26
8. Pennsylvania Turnpike	18
9. Indiana East-West	17
10. Massachusetts Turnpike	12

—From M. Hirsh Goldberg, *The Blunder Book*, Morrow, New York, 1984.

I can't say I've driven on all these highways, but #2 is definitely adding injury to insult. Which is worse, getting killed on the New Jersey Turnpike or getting off in Secaucus? Irate Garden Staters, including Bruce Springsteen, can write to me in care of the publisher.

State Line or Bust

The 10 Worst States for Driver and Pedestrian Fatalities

	Deaths/100,000 Population
1. Wyoming	51.7
2. New Mexico	47.2
3. Nevada	43.2
4. Montana	41.2
5. Arizona	34.7
5. Idaho	34.7
7. South Dakota	32.9
7. Oklahoma	32.9
9. Texas	31.0
10. Florida	29.5

—From National Safety Council 1980 statistics.

Bumper Cars

The 19 Cars with the Worst Injury Records*

1. Nissan Pulsar

2. Plymouth Colt, 4-wheel drive

3. Mitsubishi Tredia

4. Pontiac 1000, 2-door

5. Chevrolet Chevette, 2-door

6. Mitsubishi Cordia

7. Dodge Colt, 2-door

8. Plymouth Colt, 2-door

9. Toyota Starlet

10. Nissan Sentra, 4-door

11. Dodge Colt, 4-door

12. Chevrolet Chevette, 4-door

13. Honda Civic CRX

14. Isuzu T-car/I-Mark, 4-door

15. Pontiac 1000, 4-door

16. Renault Alliance, 2-door

17. Nissan Sentra, 2-door

18. Mercury Lynx, 2-door

19. Ford Mustang

*Based on the relative frequency of injury claims, 1982–1984 passenger cars.

—From the Highway Loss Data Institute.

The fact that people who own and ride in these cars get racked up more than others may not be entirely a bad sign. After all, there are plenty of Americans who love thrills. The car manu-facturers should make lemonade out of the lemons and at least provide a suitably adventuresome-sounding name—e.g., the Pulse-Stopper, the Whiplash, the Crusher, the Careener, or the Knievel. Why not let others know you live dangerously?

Catch That Bus, Don't Kiss It

*The 7 Leading Causes of Catastrophic Death in the U.S.**

	Deaths
1. Fire and explosion	13,398
2. Motor vehicles	11,040
3. Tornadoes, floods, hurricanes	9,337
4. Air transportation	8,828
5. Water transportation	2,584
6. Mines and quarries	1,668
7. Railroad transportation	1,367

*Five or more people killed at once, 1941–1980.

—From *Statistical Bulletin*, Metropolitan Life Insurance Co., April–June, 1982.

Dying Young

*The 8 Leading Causes of Accidental Death in Children Aged 1 or Under**

	Deaths/100,000 Population/Yr	
	Boys	Girls
1. Motor vehicle	10.9	11.0
2. Drowning	7.7	5.6
3. Fire and flames	5.4	5.3
4. Pedestrian	3.1	3.0
5. Inhalation/ingestion	3.0	1.8
6. Falls	1.7	1.3

| 7. Poisoning | 1.3 | 1.2 |
| 8. Drugs and medicaments | 0.6 | 0.5 |

*A third of all deaths among 1-year-olds are caused by accidents.

—From the Division of Vital Statistics, National Center for Health Statistics.

Never Too Old to Get Killed

The 8 Leading Causes of Death in Those Aged 75 and Over

	Deaths per 100,00 Population per Year	
	Men	Women
1. Falls	91.8	83.3
2. Motor vehicle	49.8	18.5
3. Pedestrian	18.1	18.5
4. Fire and flames	14.8	8.3
5. Inhalation/ingestion	10.4	6.6
6. Drowning	3.4	1.4
7. Poisoning	2.5	1.8
8. Drugs and medicaments	1.9	1.6

—From the Division of Vital Statistics, National Center for Health Statistics.

I know this sounds snide, but isn't death the cause of the fall in some of those cases? There's not much cause for levity here unless you recall the old garment worker who fell in the streets of Manhattan. A Samaritan put a pillow under his head and asked, "Are you comfortable?" The old man answered, "I make a living."

Never Too Young to Die

The 12 Worst Countries in Which to Be Born*

	Infant Deaths/ 1000 Births
1. Ethiopia	155–200
2. Afghanistan	182
3. Nigeria	178
4. Zaire	165–177
5. Morocco	162
6. Mozambique	147–150
7. Bangladesh	148
8. Sudan	140–144
9. Algeria	127
10. India	125
10. Turkey	125
12. Uganda	120

*These figures are based in 1982 statistics, which show Japan to be the best place to be born—7 deaths/1000 births. The rate in the U.S. is 11 deaths/ 1000 births.

—From the U.N. Population Division.

Nasty, Brutish, and Short

The 10 Worst Countries in Which to Try and Grow Old*

	Ave Life Expectancy, Yrs
1. Ethiopia	36–44
2. Zaire	37–40
3. Afghanistan	41
3. Nigeria	41
5. Nepal	44
6. Sudan	45–47
7. Tanzania	45–49

8. Uganda	46
9. Bangladesh	48
10. Ghana	49

*These figures are based on data submitted by 120 nations. Japan and the Netherlands boast the longest average life expectancy—76 years; the U.S. figures show 70 years for a male, 78 for a female.

—From the U.N. Population Division.

One question puzzles me about these grim statistics. If a child dies in infancy, as so many do, is it balanced by someone living to 80—hence, bringing the average to 40? That's much too simple a calculus, but it would be nice to envision someone, anyone, living a full life in the Third World.

I'd Rather Be Dead Than in...(Part I)

The 10 U.S. Cities with the Most Deaths per Year

	Deaths/Yr
1. New York, NY	73,767
2. Chicago, IL	31,828
3. Los Angeles, CA	27,031
4. Philadelphia, PA	20,711
5. Detroit, MI	14,286
6. Houston, TX	11,036
7. Baltimore, MD	9,741
8. San Francisco, CA	7,680
9. Cleveland, OH	7,469
10. Dallas, TX	7,348

—From *199 American Cities Compared*, Information Publications, Burlington, VT, 1984 (U.S. Census, 1980).

Martin Mull called Miami "God's waiting room." It seems he got it wrong; the Big Apple is the place to go rotten.

I'd Rather Be Dead Than in...(Part II)

The 10 States with the Worst Life Expectancy

		Ave Life Expectancy, Yrs
1.	South Carolina	67.96
2.	Mississippi	68.09
3.	Georgia	68.54
4.	Louisiana	68.76
5.	Nevada	69.03
6.	Alabama	69.05
7.	North Carolina	69.21
8.	Alaska	69.31
9.	West Virginia	69.48
10.	Delaware	70.06

—From Richard Boyer and David Savageau, *Places Rated Almanac*, Rand McNally, Chicago, 1985 (National Center for Health Statistics, 1969–1971, U.S. Dept. of Energy).

The Red Badge of Courage

The 5 Worst Wars for Loss of American Life

		Deaths
1.	Civil War	529,332
2.	World War II	405,399
3.	World War I	116,516
4.	Vietnam	56,962
5.	Korea	54,246

—From *Information Please Almanac, Atlas and Yearbook*, 1978.

Every one of these wars was a tragedy. But consider that the Russians lost 5 times the sum of all of these lives in World War II. I'm not making excuses for their behavior, but it must give them an entirely different perspective on the nuclear threat that we seem to accept so blithely. And we have invaded them once already.

The Good Fight (Part I)

The 9 Countries with the Worst Battle Casualties in World War I

		Deaths
1.	Germany	1,773,700
2.	Russia	1,700,000
3.	France	1,357,800
4.	Austria-Hungary	1,200,000
5.	British Empire	908,371
6.	Italy	650,000
7.	Romania	335,706
8.	Turkey	325,000
9.	United States	116,516

—From *Information Please Almanac, Atlas and Yearbook*, 1979.

Consider for a moment that the Iranians and Iraqis are piling up comparable figures right now.

The Good Fight (Part II)

The 9 Countries with the Worst Battle Casualties in World War II

		Deaths
1.	Soviet Union	6,115,000
2.	Germany	3,250,000
3.	China	1,324,516
4.	Japan	1,270,000

5. Poland	664,000
6. Britain	357,116
7. Romania	350,000
8. Yugoslavia	305,000
9. United States	291,557

—From *Information Please Almanac, Atlas and Yearbook*, 1979.

Counting civilian casualties, the figures for the Soviet Union are closer to 20 million.

Going Up in Smoke

The 10 Worst Disasters in the U.S.*

	Deaths
1. Fire and explosion, Texas City, TX, April 16–17, 1947	561
2. Nightclub fire, Boston, MA, November 28, 1942	492 ∗
3. Hurricane and floods, Louisiana, Texas, and several other states, June 27–28, 1957	395
4. Explosion of two ammunition ships, Port Chicago, CA, July 18, 1944	322
5. Series of tornadoes in midwest and south, April 3–4, 1987	307
6. Plane crash, O'Hare Airport, Chicago, IL, May 25, 1979	273
7. Series of tornadoes in midwest, April 11, 1965	272
8. Hurricane and subsequent floods, Mississippi, Louisiana, and Virginia, August 17–20, 1969	256
9. Flash flood, Rapid City, SD, June 9, 1972	237

10. Series of tornadoes, Mississippi Valley,
    March 21–22, 1952   229

*Between 1941 and 1980.

—From *Statistical Bulletin*, Metropolitan Life Insurance Co., April–June, 1982.

Under the Volcano

The 10 Worst Eruptions in History

		Deaths
1.	Krakatoa, Indonesia, August 26–27, 1883, the loudest explosion in history	36,000
2.	Mount Pelée, Martinique, West Indies, May 8, 1902	30,000
3.	Nevado del Ruiz, Armero, Colombia, November 13, 1985*	23,000
4.	Mount Vesuvius, Pompeii and Herculaneum, Italy, August 24, 79	20,000
4.	Mount Etna, Catania, Sicily, March 25, 1669	20,000
6.	Tambora, Java, April 5, 1815	10,000–12,000
7.	Skaptar, Lakagigar, Iceland, June–August 1783	10,000
8.	Mount Kelud, Indonesia, May 1919	5,000
9.	Mount Vesuvius, Italy, December 16, 1631	4,000
10.	Galunggung, Java, October 8 and 12, 1822	4,000

*With update from wire service stories.

—From James Cornell, *The Great International Disaster Book,* Scribner's, New York, 1984.

Not only was Krakatoa the worst eruption, but Krakatoa: East of Java was the worst eruption movie. The 1883 explosion blackened the sky as far away as London, a reasonable forewarning of the effects of nuclear winter.

The Tidal Wave Goodbye

The 7 Worst Tsunami in History

	Deaths
1. Krakatoa, Indonesia, August 17, 1883	36,000*
2. Japan, 1707	30,000
3. Sanriku, Japan, June 15, 1896	20,000
4. Lisbon, Portugal, November 1, 1755	10,000
5. Sanriku, Japan, 1933	3,000
6. Hilo, Hawaii, May 22, 1960	300
7. Hawaii, April 1, 1946	173

*All estimated deaths from volcanic eruption are attributed to resulting tsunami, in this estimate.

—From James Cornell, *The Great International Disaster Book*, Scribner's, New York, 1984.

Not the Way to Oz

The 10 Worst Tornadoes in History

	Deaths
1. Midwestern U.S., March 18, 1925	689
2. Southern U.S., February 9–19, 1884	600
3. Dacca, East Pakistan, April 14, 1969	540
4. Mississippi and Georgia, April 5–6, 1936	419
5. St. Louis, MO, May 27, 1896	400+
6. Southcentral U.S., March 21–22, 1952	343
7. Midwestern U.S., April 3–4, 1974	315
8. Natchez, MS, May 7, 1840	300+

9. Midwestern U.S., April 11, 1965   272
10. Alabama, March 21, 1932   268

—From James Cornell, *The Great International Disaster Book*, Scribner's, New York, 1984.

A Plague on Many Houses

The 10 Worst Epidemics in History

	Deaths, in Millions
1. Europe and Asia (plague), 500–650	≈100
2. Western Europe (Black Death), 1347–1351	75
3. The world (Spanish influenza), 1918–1919	25–50
4. India (plague), 1898–1923	11–12
5. Eastern Europe (typhus), 1914–1915	3
6. Mezzo-America (smallpox), 1500 and after	*
7. Western Europe (syphilis), 1500 and after	*
8. England (English sweats), 1485–1550	2+
9. Mexico (measles), 1530–1545	1–1.5
10. India (malaria), 1947	1

*Figures (in the millions) not available.

—From James Cornell, *The Great International Disaster Book*, Scribner's, New York, 1984.

The figures on AIDS are not in; by the next century those figures may well dwarf them all. But who will be left to record them?

Land Oh!

The 10 Worst Landslides in History

	Deaths
1. Kansu, China, December 16, 1920	180,000
2. Khait, Tadzhikistan, 1949	12,000
3. Chiavenna Valley, Italy	2,420
4. Rio de Janeiro, Brazil, January 11–13, 1966	550
5. Goldau Valley, Switzerland, September 2, 1806	500
6. Huancavelica province, Peru, April 26, 1974	200–300
7. Los Angeles, CA, March 2, 1938	200+
8. Nebukawa, Japan, September 1, 1923	200
8. Chungar, Peru, March 18, 1971	200
8. Eastern Colombia, June 28, 1974	200

—From James Cornell, *The Great International Disaster Book*, Scribner's, New York, 1984.

Air Chance

The 10 Worst Airplane Crashes in History

	Deaths
1. Collision of two Boeing 747s, Tenerife airport, Canary Islands, March 1977	582
2. Crash of a Japan Airlines 747 into a Japanese hillside, August 13, 1985	520
3. Crash of a Turkish DC-10 northeast of Paris, March 1974	346
4. Crash of an Air India 747 off the coast of Ireland, June 23, 1985	329
5. Fiery emergency landing of a Saudi Arabian L-1011 jet at Riyadh airport, August 19, 1980	301

6. Crash of an American Airlines DC-10 on takeoff, Chicago, May 25, 1979 — 273
7. Korean Air Lines 747 shot down by Soviet fighter, near Sakhalin Island, U.S.S.R., September 1, 1983 — 269
8. Crash of a chartered Arrow Airlines flight on takeoff from Gander Air Force Base, Newfoundland, December 17, 1985 — 258
9. Crash of an Air New Zealand DC-10, Antarctica, November 1979 — 257
10. Crash of an Air India 747 on takeoff, Bombay, January 1, 1978 — 213

—From the Associated Press.

Torpedo the Dams

The 10 Worst Floods in History

	Deaths
1. Hwang Ho (Yellow) River, China, September–October 1887	900,000
2. North China, 1939	500,000
3. Shantung Peninsula, People's Republic of China, April 23, 1969 (Japanese reporters claim several hundred thousand deaths)	*
4. Kaifeng, Hunan Province, China, 1642	300,000+
5. England and the Netherlands, 1099 (Records are questionable)	≈100,000
6. The Netherlands, December 14, 1287	50,000
7. Neva River, Russia, 1824	10,000
7. The Netherlands, November 18, 1421	10,000
9. Mekong Delta, South Vietnam, November–December, 1964	5,000

10. Manchuria, August 6–7, 1951 4,800

*Figures not available.

—From James Cornell, *The Great International Disaster Book*, Scribner's, New York, 1984.

No Time to Say Grace

The 10 Worst Famines in History

	Deaths, Millions
1. North China, 1876–1879 (hunger accompanied by violence and disease, the worst human disaster in modern times)	9–13
2. India, 1876–1879 (3.5 million died in Madras alone)	5
2. India, 1896–1897	5
4. Soviet Union, 1932–1934	*
5. India, 1769–1770	3
5. China, 1928–1929	3
7. Soviet Union, 1921–1922	1.2–5
8. Bengal, India, 1899–1900	1.25–3.25
9. India, 1943–1944	1.5
10. Ireland, 1846–1851 (great potato famine, which also led 1 million to emigrate)	1

*Figures not available.

—From James Cornell, *The Great International Disaster Book*, Scribner's, New York, 1984.

Naturalists like author-photographer Peter Beard contend that famine will be exacerbated by our feeding of populations in overburdened, denuded habitats. Politics blocks migration and de-

velopment, so what choice do we have? This is one of the worst conundrums we will face or ignore in the near future.

Shake, Rattle, and Kill

The 10 Worst Earthquakes in History

		Deaths
1.	Shensi province, China, January 23, 1556	830,000+
2.	Calcutta, India, October 11, 1737	300,000
3.	Tangshan, China, July 28, 1976	242,000
4.	Kansu, China, December 16, 1920	180,000
5.	Tokyo-Yokohama, Japan, September 1, 1923	140,000
6.	Gulf of Chihli, China, September 27, 1290	100,000
6.	Peking, China, 1731	100,000
8.	Messina, Italy, December 28, 1908	75,000–85,000
9.	Naples, Italy, 1693	90,000
10.	Shemakha, Caucasia, November 1667	80,000

—From James Cornell, *The Great International Disaster Book*, Scribner's, New York, 1984.

Whirling 'Round and 'Round

The 10 Worst Cyclones in History

Deaths

1. East Pakistan, November 13, 1970   1,000,000
2. Bengal, India, October 7, 1737   300,000
2. Haiphong, Vietnam, 1881   300,000
4. Bengal, India, 1876 (100,000 killed by cyclone, 100,000 by starvation)   200,000
5. Bombay, India, June 6, 1882   100,000
6. Calcutta, India, October 5, 1864   50,000–70,000
7. East Pakistan, May 1–12, June 1–2, 1965   35,000–40,000
8. Bengal, India, October 16, 1942   11,000–40,000
9. Caribbean Islands, October 10–12, 1780   20,000–30,000
10. East Pakistan, May 28–29, 1963   22,000

—From James Cornell, *The Great International Disaster Book*, Scribner's, New York, 1984.

Look Out Below

The 10 Worst Avalanches in History

Deaths

1. Mount Huascaran, Yungay, Peru, May 31, 1970. Millions of tons of ice and snow broke loose in the aftermath of the worst earthquake in western hemispheric history.   20,000
2. A series of avalanches in Tyrol, Italian-Austrian Alps, December 13, 1916. The death toll occurred among Italian and Austrian soldiers during a 24-hour period.   10,000
3. Mount Huascaran, Ranrahirca, Peru, January 10, 1962. The preceding day's snowfall triggered 3-ton avalanches.   3,500

4. Plurs, Switzerland, September 4, 1618. The Rodi avalanche obliterated the town and all its inhabitants except 4 who were away that day.   1,500

5. Blons, Austria, January 12, 1954. Over 200 initially died when the Falv dry-snow avalanche destroyed the central section of Blons. Some 115 rescue workers died 9 hours later when a second avalanche, the Montclav, struck the town after traveling 3000 feet in less than 30 seconds.   315

6. Alpine region, Europe, 1950–1951. This was a series of avalanches over a 3-month period, the "winter of terror."   265

7. Lahoul Valley, India, 1979. Five days of heavy snows triggered an avalanche in Himachel Pradesh. A 15- to 20-foot wall of snow killed 200 people.   200

8. Wellington, WA, March 1, 1910. Three passenger trains sat snowbound at the station house leading to Stevens Pass in Cascade Range. An avalanche roared into the pass, sweeping locomotives, several carriages, and the station house into a canyon 150 feet below.   118

9. Obergestein, Rhone Valley, Germany, 1720. The Galen avalanche destroyed 100 buildings and 400 head of cattle in the village.   88

10. Saas, Switzerland, 1689. The popular resort town in Pratigau Valley was hardest hit by avalanches that swept the Alps in 1689. Two slides from Calmut Peak on the same day destroyed 155 buildings.   73

—From James Cornell, *The Great International Disaster Book*, Scribner's, New York, 1984.

Bear in mind that even if all was lost for those caught in the tragedies listed on this and preceding pages, at least Hollywood has profited from several of them. Comforting, no?

TO THE READER

"It ain't over till it's over," to cite another dubious Yogi Berra-ism. Or was it Stengel? You made it this far, but there are always new worsts. You may be making those new nadirs yourself. After all, bad things do happen to good people. If so, and if this little number doesn't end up on remainder shelves, there may be a sequel, not to mention the clothing line, the children's toys, and the feature-length film, though I am advised, even by sales reps for this company, not to hold my breath.

So write to us when you've observed or made worst-in-life status. The guys at Guinness can't use everything, after all. If we have another go-round, you'll get a T-shirt or a trip to the Anderson of your choice, not to mention our gratitude.

Send your worsts to *The Worst of Everything*, P.O. Box 481, Harvard, MA 01451. And break a leg.

Catalog

If you are interested in a list of fine Paperback
books, covering a wide range of subjects
and interests, send your name and address,
requesting your free catalog, to:

McGraw-Hill Paperbacks
11 West 19th Street
New York, N.Y. 10011